PATTERNS *from* PARADISE

Overleaf:
A Tahitian woman appliqués
a breadfruit, or *uru*, design to
a quilt, using tiny overcast
stitches.

PATTERNS *from* PARADISE

The Art of Tahitian Quilting

Vicki Poggioli

THE MAIN STREET PRESS • Pittstown, New Jersey

For John and Jim

Published by
The Main Street Press, Inc.
William Case House
Pittstown, New Jersey 08867

Published simultaneously in Canada by
McGraw-Hill Ryerson Ltd.
330 Progress Avenue
Scarborough, Ontario MIP 2Z5

Cover design by Robert Reed
Text design by Ronald R. Misiur
Photographs by John Poggioli and Vicki Poggioli
Printed in Japan

Library of Congress Cataloging-in-Publication Data

Poggioli, Vicki.
  Patterns from paradise.

  Bibliography: p.
  1. Quilting—Society Islands—Tahiti—Patterns.
2. Appliqué—Society Islands—Tahiti—Patterns.
3. Tahiti—Social life and customs. I. Title.
TT835.P64 1988   746.9'7'0996211   88-10010
ISBN 1-55562-052-3 (pbk.)
ISBN 1-55562-077-9 (cloth)

88 89 90 91 92   10 9 8 7 6 5 4 3 2 1

Contents

Introduction   7

1. **Tifaifai: A Cultural Journey**   13

2. **From Heart to Hand**   21

3. **Design: A Polynesian Perspective**   29

4. **A Gallery of Tahitian Designs**   48

   Te Vahine e te Miti, *The Woman and the Sea*   51

   Aute, *Hibiscus*   56

   Uru, *Breadfruit*   60

   Roti (A), *Rose*   64

   Chou, *Cabbage*   69

   Tifaifai Pu, *Patchwork*   73

   Tiare Tahiti, *Gardenia*   77

   Orchide   81

   Roti (B), *Rose*   87

   Tahirihiri, *Fans*   91

   Te Mori, *The Lamp*   95

   Anthuriums   98

   Hei Tiare, *Floral Wreath*   105

   Pūpū, *Shells*   109

   Te Moemoea no Itoefa, *Joseph's Dream*   113

Pronunciation Guide   117

Glossary   118

Bibliography   121

Acknowledgments   123

Index   125

Introduction

Halfway between the Australian continent and the California coastline, in the vastness of the blue Pacific, are the emerald islands of Tahiti, the mecca of the South Seas. Tahiti is the island of legends. It is the land of white sand beaches, lapis lazuli waters, sensuous women, and easy living. The imagery connected with Tahiti has brought adventurers of every sort to these islands. Beachcombers, whalers, missionaries, painters, and writers have made their way to Tahiti in search of something better. Some were seeking an easy life. Some sought freedom from the cold "civilized" nations of the north. And some were seeking paradise.

Paradise. In any society, an earthly paradise can only be an illusion. But the Tahitian environment—a comforting blend of warm days and gentle nights, lush vegetation, azure lagoons, rainbows, and rain—can be described as a kind of paradise. This environment has inspired many artists, from the very famous Paul Gauguin to the unknown Tahitian artisan who makes quilts based on the patterns of nature.

There is a startling play of light in the islands that makes colors seem to throb and glow from within. Exotic flowers dot the landscape in shades of red, yellow, coral, and pink. Gauguin, the post-impressionist painter who lived and worked in Tahiti, wrote in his journal, *Noa Noa*, ". . . it was so simple to paint things as I saw them, to put without special calculation a red close to a blue." The truth of his observation can be seen just about everywhere. Pink painted outriggers float in blue lagoons. Magenta bougainvillaea grow alongside pale-yellow frangipani. Crimson hibiscus are set against brown Tahitian skin.

The red hibiscus is a symbol of the islands and is often worn as a hair ornament.

The often brash and impulsive color combinations found in Tahitian quilts can be attributed to their creators' observations of nature. As did Gauguin, the quilter simply sets down what is there.

But why quilts in tropical Tahiti? When viewed from the perspective of the chilly northern hemisphere, Tahitian quilts do not seem functional. The weather is hot. The islands are situated near the equator. Tahitian quilts, known as *tifaifai*, are made for two reasons: first, they fill a cultural void left by the imposition of Western material culture and, second, they are made sheerly for beauty and pleasure. Quilting was introduced to Tahiti by Europeans, but is now something that belongs to the Tahitian people. It is the special métier of Tahitian artisans and is a tangible link with the Polynesian past.

The tifaifai came about as a result of the European and American presence in the South Pacific. Once introduced by missionaries, the techniques, patterns, and motifs spread throughout the islands of Polynesia. The people of Rarotonga and Aitutaki in the Cook Islands, Rurutu and Tubuai in the Austral

A Rarotongan woman now living in Tahiti wears the traditional *hei*, a wreath of flowers around her head.

Islands, the Hawaiian Islands, and little known places like Niue, received instruction in sewing and quilting, too. Regional styles developed according to the particular methods taught by missionaries in each archipelago. These new skills were also spread by so-called "native teachers," Polynesians who took the gospel and the technology of the missionaries upon themselves and brought them to far-flung islands where missionaries did not go. Other overlooked influences in sewing and quilting may have come from the wives of whaling captains who sailed on ships known as "hen frigates." These women spent years at sea, they were familiar with South Seas ports, and passed the time at sea with needle and thread. Even the sailors themselves may have had a hand in spreading sewing skills among Polynesians. Every ship had a supply of needles, thread, and cloth for the crew. Sailors were known to make quilts during voyages that often lasted several years.

There is a frustrating lack of documentation concerning the introduction and development of Tahitian quilting. Polynesians did not keep written histories, but, instead, kept oral histories that were committed to memory through songs, chants, and dances. If a big battle was fought, a song was composed, and in that way it was recorded in the Tahitian memory. Early missionaries and visitors to Tahiti were predominantly male and had little interest in the development of needlework among Polynesian women. Yankee missionaries in Hawaii kept better records, but even these writings were few and far between. There is almost no written work concerning the Tahitian quilt. Among the exceptions, however, are a few notes made by women of the mid-1800s; an article by Patrick O'Reilly written in 1959, "Note sur les Tifaifai Tahitiens," for the *Journal de la Société des Océanistes*; and a wonderful book about Polynesian quilting written in 1986 by Joyce Hammond, *Tifaifai and Quilts of Polynesia*.

Much of the information about the early development and forms of the Tahitian quilt that I collected has come from the lips of the women who make tifaifai. These bits of information were passed down from mothers, aunts, and grandmothers and are widely known among the artisans. There is a surprising uniformity to the stories about early tifaifai. Many of the artisans "know" that patchwork was done by their ancestors in the 1700s, despite the absence of any documentation to confirm this. Because the usual avenues of research are mostly closed, it is my belief that the recollections of the Tahitian people are the best resource of all.

On first examination, the motifs and patterns of the appliquéd tifaifai may be hard to visualize. The quilts are unusually large, averaging eight feet by seven feet, and the designs are unfamiliar. Most designs are based on the flora of the islands and, to the untrained eye, may be unrecognizable. Something akin to a "right brain" shift is necessary to see and comprehend the spatial relationships of some of the patterns. But the basic technique is a simple one, based on snowflake-like designs made of folded paper.

Although the basis of the tifaifai is simple, making the quilts is not always easy. Certainly, some prior experience with appliqué is necessary. Tahitian women have a sure and practiced touch when making tifaifai. They reject the fussy steps and tend to simplify the process whenever possible. Some women choose not to pin, feeling that pins get in the way. Some take shortcuts with basting. Others draw designs without patterns of any kind. The many curves in the designs are not hemmed, pressed, or notched before appliqué, due to the large size of the motifs. If you are unfamiliar with the techniques necessary in making large-scale appliqué designs, you should take all the usual precautions of pinning and basting in order to make these quilts successfully.

New forms of tifaifai have appeared in recent years. Printed fabrics, once found only in some patchwork quilts, are now used in the big appliquéd designs. Painted tifaifai and pillowslips are also being made. But, most women consider them too far from the Tahitian tradition and they are not popular. The traditional forms of patchwork and appliqué are preferred by most Tahitian artisans and consumers.

When in Tahiti, the casual tourist often has difficulty finding examples of tifaifai. Unless there is an exhibition in progress or unless one of the government-sponsored craft centers is nearby, the tifaifai will prove to be illusive. The best tifaifai, the masterpieces, are rarely seen, but remain in the home, brought out only for important occasions. Old tifaifai, dating back to the turn of the century or earlier, are extremely difficult to find. One reason is that the Tahitians are not collectors of antiques. Secondly,

Tiare Opuhi, a native Tahitian flower, is a favorite theme for tifaifai.

the effect of heat, humidity, and insects on fabric can be devastating. Most visitors to the islands must content themselves with a glimpse of a tifaifai on a clothesline in Moorea. Or a tifaifai under construction in a backyard in Bora Bora. Or a faded tifaifai wrapped around children asleep in the back of a pickup truck.

Because of the annual exhibitions of traditional arts and crafts held in July in the district of Pirae and the city of Papeete, I was able to photograph a number of the quilts for this book. Although several styles of tifaifai and many patterns are represented here, there are many, many more that I was unable to photograph. The tifaifai is more than a quilt, you see. It is an embodiment of the Tahitian way of life, the Tahitian heart, and the pride of the Tahitian past. A woman does not share a gift of a tifaifai or its designs or its methods easily. She thinks about it. She looks you square in the eye. She consults

A booth at the craft village in Pirae. Three styles of tifaifai are hung on the walls. From right to left: a quilt in the Hawaiian style, another in the Rarotongan style, and a third in one of the several Tahitian styles.

with a friend, or her husband, or the president of her craft association and then, maybe, she allows you to share in its secrets.

This is the first book on how to make Tahitian quilts. In the following pages, the introduction to quilting in Tahiti and the subsequent evolution of tifaifai are examined. Also included are the ways that tifaifai are used in traditional Tahitian culture. The design chapter is both an overview of the different styles of tifaifai and a visual introduction to the quilts. The project chapter offers commentary and instructions for fifteen additional quilts.

This book could not have been written without the remarkable kindness of the artisans who make tifaifai. When making tifaifai for your home or your loved ones, know and remember that what you are making is very precious, indeed. The generosity, hospitality, and kindness of the Tahitian people is legendary. I have always found this to be true. My thanks to the artisans and the people of Tahiti for sharing these very special quilts. *Mauruuru.*

A very common scene in the Pirae craft village. The artisans take a break from work for some festive traditional dancing.

1. Tifaifai: A Cultural Journey

When the visiting queen of Tonga arrived in Tahiti in July, 1987, to celebrate the observance of Bastille Day, she was brought to the village of artisans. She was welcomed by long lines of singing matrons and the rich a cappella harmonies of Tahitian chants. The women wore long gowns in bright tropical colors. Wreaths of leaves, flowers, and shells were draped around their shoulders and on their heads. One elderly woman, dressed in a stark white "missionary" dress, danced a slow hula down the human passageway to formally greet the Tongan queen. The queen was led to a shady platform and seated in a chair that was covered with a Tahitian quilt, a tifaifai, of hot pink on a pale pink background. Beneath her feet were finely woven mats of pandanus and palm. Songs were sung. Speeches were made. And then six women stepped onto the platform in front of the queen. In their hands was a sky-blue tifaifai, covered with mermaids and shells made of a deeper blue cloth. The women deftly opened the overlarge quilt and, half bowing in deference to Her Majesty, slowly advanced and displayed the beauty of the design. The queen of Tonga stood. She was then tightly wrapped in the tifaifai, from neck to feet, on this unusually hot and steamy afternoon.

Several days later the queen returned. Her attendants produced, from the trunk of a black Cadillac, a thick bolt of tapa, the bark cloth made in her home islands. The tapa was a rich and even brown with hand-painted black geometric designs that shone and glistened in the sunshine. A soft gasp rippled through the cluster of women who gathered around the queen. The meaning of the tapa was clear. It matched exactly, in form and value, the gift of the blue tifaifai.

Quilting came late to Tahiti. For centuries fine mats and tapa were used as ceremonial markers for the most important occasions of life. Although tapa, known locally as *ahu*, and fine mats were put to work in everyday life as floor coverings, bedding, and clothing, the finest examples of this work were rarely used. The best were stored away as a form of wealth or given away to express the deepest respect or love.

In the Samoan islands, considered the homeland of Polynesian culture, the women still weave soft, flexible mats from strips of pandanus. Each strip measures an eighth of an inch wide or less. The mats are sometimes worn around the waist for special occasions, or they are stored in bundles as a form of currency. The customs surrounding fine mats remain strong. Even today, if a wrong has been committed between clans, it is possible to win forgiveness by offering fine mats to the offended party. If the mats are accepted, the debt is paid. Some of the oldest mats, made generations ago, are given names and carry long histories.

The use of fine mats and tapa for clothing was a tradition in Polynesia before quilting was known. Treasured fine mats are displayed by these Samoan women. The woman in front is wearing a mat around her waist. In the middle, a woman is girdled with a piece of tapa barkcloth.

Tongan islanders hold tapa in similiar esteem. Tapa-bark cloth is the cement that holds the culture together. It is made by groups of women and is a necessary ingredient in ceremonies commemorating all the milestones of life, from birth to death. Bundles of tapa are considered to be a form of wealth, much like the mats of Samoa. Tapa is part of every bride's dowry. During the coronation of Tonga's king in the 1960s, villagers laid immense sheets of tapa on the streets of the capital city to express their respect for the new king and his family.

In ancient Tahiti, the wealth and status of a chief was once measured by the bales of tapa he owned. Tapa was used to wrap a sacred temple relic, an honored guest, or a high chief. Today, the honored individual is wrapped with a tifaifai. Although the Pacific islands of Samoa, Tonga, and Tahiti are distant from one another and are culturally diverse, there is an older, underlying Polynesian culture that recognizes the value and interrelationship of these handicrafts. Joining Pacific islanders together with each other and a common heritage is a beautiful braid of three parts—tapa, mats, and tifaifai.

It was only two centuries ago that needlework and quilting made an appearance in Polynesia. English missionaries brought the skills with them to the islands. On March 5, 1797, a tall sailing ship dropped anchor in Matavai Bay, off the coast of Tahiti. The ship was the *HMS Duff*, a missionary ship from England. Tahiti had been discovered in 1767 by a British exploration team. Among the European captains who subsequently dropped anchor off Tahiti were Captain James Cook in 1769 and Captain William Bligh on board the ill-fated *Bounty* in 1788. It was the writings of these men, particularly Captain Cook, that inspired the *Duff*'s eighteen young missionaries to settle in Tahiti and leave all they knew far behind them in England.

There were six women on board the *Duff*. These were everyday women, missionary wives, well versed in hard work and the domestic arts. These were the women who introduced quilting to the Tahitians. Missionary wives of that era had no official function but to assist their husbands. Even so, they made enormous contributions. Wherever missionary women went in the Pacific, they zealously taught needlework and quilting. Over the years as more missionaries came to the South Pacific, quilting skills spread throughout the islands, among them the Austral islands, the Hawaiian islands, and even the Samoan and Tongan islands. However, quilting never supplanted the use of tapa and mats in Samoa and Tonga and was largely rejected by the islanders there.

Before the arrival of Europeans in Tahiti, there was no woven cloth. Instead, the islanders made tapa from the tender inner bark of mulberry and breadfruit saplings. The bark was first stripped, then soaked in water, and pounded out on flattened logs with grooved and patterned mallets. Repeated and rhythmic pounding by the tapa beaters blended the fibers together until the end result was a fabric with the consistency of felt. The colors of tapa ranged from dark brown to brilliant white according to the type of bark that was used. Designs were painted on or stamped on with vegetable dyes. Ferns, leaves, and flowers such as hibiscus were saturated with the dyes and then impressed on the borders of the tapa in lacy and delicate patterns. This novel border work set Tahitian tapa apart from other Polynesian varieties and is considered by many Tahitians to be a forerunner of contemporary appliqués found on tifaifai.

Once settled on the island, the missionaries found that the Tahitian people had little interest in their Christian religion. But there was immediate interest in the technology they brought with them. Technical skill and quality craftsmanship were highly respected in Tahitian society. The finest tapa was made by the female *arii*, the royal wives of high chiefs, and by male priests for use in sacred rites. But there was a problem with tapa. Repeated exposure to water caused it to disintegrate. Trade cloth and the missionaries' expertise in needlework were immediately perceived by the chiefs as valuable new tools.

There is little documentation in the historical record concerning the particulars of such "women's work." However, the quick intelligence and curiosity of the Tahitian people, coupled with missionary zeal, probably led to the very early introduction of sewing and quilting, perhaps before 1800. In April, 1820, in the Hawaiian islands, an impromptu sewing lesson took place on the deck of a missionary ship. Before missionaries were permitted to go ashore, they first had to teach high-born Hawaiian women elementary piecework. If the Hawaiian introduction to quilting can be an example, it seems likely that the Tahitians learned the new and highly regarded skills almost immediately. Royal Tahitian women were certainly no less curious or demanding than their Hawaiian counterparts. Hawaiian quilts are often considered the forerunners of Polynesian quilts. However, missionaries didn't arrive in Hawaii until 1820. In Tahiti, during the same year, the demand for cloth was so high that newly introduced cotton crops were being grown. In 1821, weaving and carding machines were in place in Tahiti to make the locally grown cotton into cloth. With this in mind, it seems most likely that Polynesian piecework quilts were first made in Tahiti.

The early endeavors of missionaries were interrupted by tribal wars that raged through the islands. Many of the original missionaries fled Tahiti for New South Wales and safety. One historian notes that "four pious young women" had to be sent to Tahiti to relieve the shortage of marriageable women. By the time the wars ended in 1815, only one missionary remained. Eighteen fifteen was the year that the first Christian convert—King Pomare II—was made.

With Pomare's conversion, Christianity swept through the islands. Missionary authority and European values became dominant in both the religious and secular sides of life. During the years of peace, waves of missionaries came to Tahiti. Most were British, but, later, Americans and French came to Tahiti and undoubtedly brought their own regional sewing skills with them. Tapa making came under restrictions among the new Tahitian converts. Tapa had always been made under the auspices of the goddess Hina, who was a kind of patron saint. The missionaries believed that "idle hands are the devil's workshop" and believed just as strongly that the path to salvation lay in the mastery of "civilized" skills. European-style domestic arts were therefore taught in earnest. William Ellis, a missionary of those early years, noted that by 1830 the average Tahitian woman spent much of her day engaged in needlework instead of tapa beating. Tapa craft did not disappear quickly, however, and tapa was made well into the twentieth century.

The earliest quilts were patchwork. Patchwork was taught as a beginner's technique, as it had been in England when children began needlework instruction this way. But close on the heels of patchwork was appliqué. When considering the strict social stratification of old Tahitian society, it is clear that patchwork and appliqué could have evolved together along parallel lines. While the general population made do with what trade cloth they could get and used it for tiny patches, the households of the chiefs had access to more and better cloth. Appliqué, by definition, required more fabric than was available to the average Tahitian.

The patchwork done by Tahitian women was called *pu*. High-necked "Mother Hubbard" dresses were the primary medium for original Tahitian patchwork. These garments were sent over by mission societies in England, cast-offs from well-to-do ladies. Many were made of wool and were too hot to wear. Others were ragged and unsightly. These dresses were transformed into tiny patches, squares, rectangles, and, especially, hexagons.

"I learned on little patches." So says an eighty-one-year-old woman from the island of Bora Bora. "My grandmother and aunty made me sew something very small. Six-sided or eight-sided patches that formed little flowers. If the stitches were poor, my grandmother would tear them out, iron them flat, and I started all over. We appliquéd the little flowers to another fabric, sometimes blocks, sometimes a whole sheet of cloth. My grandmother told me that the old colors for this kind of tifaifai were red and white or blue and white."

Hexagons were popular from the earliest times. The Tahitians named them *pa'a honu,* or turtle, because of the similarity of shape between a hexagon and the shell of a sea turtle. This renaming of patterns was common in the islands and helped to make the patterns more Tahitian, more their own. Paper was not used to form the hexagons in the English piecing style, as paper was even more scarce in Tahiti than fabric.

Early pieced tifaifai were often very small. Fabric was in short supply at times and merchant ships were unreliable. The predominant colors of tifaifai pu were red and white. A bright red cloth known as "Turkey red" was highly favored among the Tahitians. It was also the most available cloth and was used as barter by merchant seamen when trading with islanders. One of the few historical notes concerning Tahitian tifaifai came from a woman of the 1850s. According to Patrick O'Reilly in his article *Note*

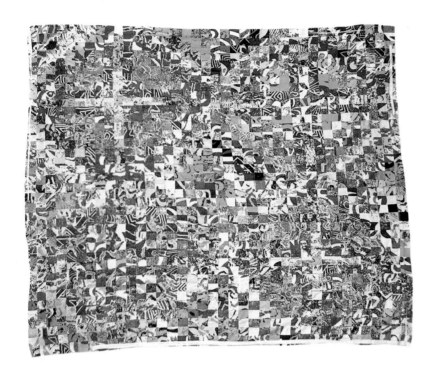

A treasured old tifaifai called "Horoi" or handkerchief, this quilt was made between 1907 and 1911 and was originally framed with a straight white border. Much skill was used to turn the many printed patterns into an organized whole. The design is said to be among the earliest taught by English missionaries. The cloth is Indonesian batik and the colors include brown, yellow, pink, red, orange, blue, white, green, and a patch or two of black. *Owned by Florence Paiea.*

sur les Tifaifai Tahitiens, Mrs. Pratt, the wife of an American Mormon missionary, came to Papeete, saw the quilts, and is thought to have been the first to describe them in writing. She noted that patchwork patterns were intricate, that quilts were beautifully made, and that all seemed to be made in two colors, red and white.

Tahitian piecework was commonly created by groups of women. Communal work habits among island women, especially in tapa making, went back to ancient times. Methods differed from the typical Western-style quilting bee. In the West, one woman usually pieced together a quilt top which was then quilted with the cooperation of several women. Or women made blocks which were later joined and quilted. In Polynesia, the tifaifai pu was made of two layers and required no quilting stitches. It was the quilt top itself that was jointly made. Repeating blocks were unpopular; larger overall patterns were preferred, patterns like Trip Around the World or mosaics with repeating elements.

Instead of dividing the tifaifai into blocks, the designer who visualized the pattern sectioned it off into eight segments, or less often, into four. When pieced, each section was a triangular shape. Four triangles made up the central design. The other four triangles formed the outer edges of the quilt. Piecing began with one corner patch, built out into diagonal rows that averaged eighty-four rows per section. The tiny scraps that made up each section were organized and strung on thread one at a time, like beads on a string, and were distributed to each woman to complete. These sections were later joined into a whole. The designer of a given quilt must posess extraordinary skills to visualize and organize the patterns and colors correctly on each string to avoid mistakes. This method is still used today.

While the majority of Tahitian women made piecework tifaifai, a preference for appliqué developed among the arii and led to a phenomenon of royal patterns. Dates are hard to come by, but the oral histories of some Tahitian women indicate that members of royal households began making appliquéd tifaifai between 1830 and 1850. This corresponds to the arrival of French colonists who replaced the British missionaries and consuls in the early 1840s. French women had a reputation for fine appliquéd work, and they may have influenced and strengthened the appliqué styles already introduced by British missionaries. Appliqué patterns created by high-born Tahitians were considered secret designs. The patterns were passed on only through members of royal households and were not made by the common people. English missionary women of that era were well versed in applique techniques and most likely were the first to introduce them to Tahitian women. Broderie perse, the intricate cutouts of India chintz, and cut paper snowflake designs were the rage among women of eighteenth-century England, and if quilts of these types were not brought with them, the knowledge of how to make them was certainly conveyed. Because English women preferred appliqué to patchwork, appliqué would have interested the women of royal households.

Although appliqué techniques were probably introduced by English missionaries, many present-day Tahitians believe that appliqué had already been known in Tahiti. Long before European influences, two special tapa garments were made in Tahiti. One was the *tiputa*, a poncho-style garment worn by men. The other was the *ahufara*, a large square shawl, worn by women. These tapa garments were richly dyed and were decorated with stamped-on borderwork and both regular and irregular floral impressions stamped at the center. William Ellis, an observant missionary, noted that some of the shawls were very large and looked more like "counterpanes," or quilts, than articles of clothing. The fancy stamped-on work found on this kind of tapa was itself a form of "laying on" and can be seen as an early form of appliqué. Appliqué quilting, already glimpsed by the Tahitians in their own early tapa work, appears to have been a logical progression, requiring changes in material and technique, rather than a conceptual change. It was, in a sense, familiar.

As Tahitian women became more adept at sewing and as fabric became more widely available, women gravitated to the more familiar appliqué style and adapted that method to their own Tahitian style and vision. Early appliqué was known as tifaifai *pa'oti*, which refers to cutting or scissors. Cutouts were small in scale, in keeping with the European method, but patterns gradually became larger and more flowing, until the entire face of the tifaifai was one large lacy design. The large connected patterns were produced by folding and cutting the fabric in the snowflake style. Patterns reflected island flora, much as they had in tapa work. Family designs emerged. One woman made up a pattern depicting breadfruit, another hibiscus, another taro, and these designs were considered the property of each family alone. Some borrowing of patterns occurred between islands. In Hawaii designs of similiar type began to appear during the same period (1830-1850). But in both appliqué and patchwork, original designs were considered secret.

This feeling of secrecy about tifaifai patterns persists today. Many women who sell their tifaifai for a living are willing to talk about their designs but refuse to share their patterns with others or allow them to be photographed. This is true even with old established patterns, if they have a slight original twist. One elderly woman who makes old piecework tifaifai of hexagons and French eagles feels that those designs belong only to her, even though she admits the patterns are very old and go back to missionary times. Some artisians say that their designs are original and are registered or copyrighted. This is most often heard in reference to appliqué patterns. When asked how this registration is done, they can not or will not say. In a gathering of well over a hundred tifaifai artisans, nearly one-third felt this strong tradition of secrecy and would not participate in any sharing of designs. As one artisan put it, "If you like my pattern, you buy my pattern."

Most contemporary tifaifai are done in appliqué style and are made of wide seamless sheets of cotton fabric. These special sheets are found in the myriad fabric shops in Tahiti's capital city of Papeete. On smaller islands, the material for tifaifai may have to be specially ordered. Before the large seamless sheets became available, artisans bought material by the yard and sewed three widths together to make one large surface. This was done for the base fabric and the applied top. Women then began experimenting with bedsheets, but colors were limited to white and a few pastels. Now the special seamless fabrics are cut in eight-foot by seven-foot dimensions, sometimes larger. They come in a spectrum of colors and are usually made of one hundred percent cotton, although cotton blends are offered. The blends, however, are considered inferior by Tahitian women. Two sheets are needed and at this writing cost approximately $25 to $30 U.S. currency per sheet.

This quilt pattern is Liane de Cyre, the Tahitian wedding flower. Traditionally worn in the hair and carried as part of the bridal bouquet, the flower blooms in December. *Quilt made by Sophie Aro.*

Templates are sometimes used for pattern guides. The templates are placed on top of folded cloth and the designs will be cut four at a time.

2. From Heart to Hand

A ny affair of the heart can turn into an opportunity to use tifaifai. In Tahiti, as in many other islands of eastern Polynesia, tifaifai are used to celebrate the most important occasions, whether affairs of state or the birthday of a beloved grandchild. To be wrapped in a tifaifai is to be wrapped in warmth, respect, acceptance, and love. Despite twentieth-century pressures on Tahitian life and what some term the "money culture," tifaifai continue to be recognized by all as honored symbols that reflect the old Polynesian ways.

In keeping with island traditions, tifaifai are widely used in marriage festivities. Wedding ceremonies are standard, taking place in city hall or in church, or both. But it is after the wedding that tifaifai come into the spotlight. The reception hall, called the *fare tamaara'a,* may be decorated with multiple tifaifai strung about the walls and ceilings, forming a dizzying canopy of color. On some islands the reception may take place outside in a tent constructed of many tifaifai lashed together. Customs vary from island to island. In Rurutu, several hundred miles from Tahiti, the *mamas* line up with tifaifai, holding them up in display and making a long passageway. Then they walk all around the couple, draping the tifaifai around them until they are piled up. In Rarotonga, one of the Cook Islands, tifaifai are used similarly to honor the new couple. They may be piled up in front of the newlyweds in a dazzling display. "So many, so beautiful, so many colors, your eyes will pop," said one Rarotongan artisan of the colorful effect.

Tahitian custom calls for the new couple to be wrapped up together in a large tifaifai. This quilt is usually made by the family of the bride or groom. Wedding tifaifai are usually made in appliqué style as was customary in the days when fabric was scarce and appliquéd tifaifai were considered the most precious. While the couple is wrapped up, the pastor who performed the marriage ceremony sometimes gives the couple a new name to mark their passage into another part of life. This wrapping up in tifaifai goes back to pre-missionary times when marriages were consecrated by using tapa. At that time, the bride and groom sat on a specially-made piece of brilliant white tapa. The ceremony was completed when another piece of white tapa was placed over the heads of the couple. This tapa was called *tapo'i* and was considered to have sacred properties. To actually place the tifaifai over the heads of newlyweds would be unusual today, but the use of tifaifai and the construction of a canopy of quilts closely resembles the old practices.

Among the beginnings celebrated with tifaifai are births and first birthdays. Historically, white tapa was given to newborns. On the first birthday, the child was honored with a bolt of bark cloth or a bundle of fine mats. In Samoa, special baby mats are still made, and the baby may spend much of his first year on such a mat near his mother. In Tahiti the tradition has become one of specially-made tifaifai for the newborn. These crib-sized quilts are considered an important part of every infant's layette. Baby tifaifai are predominantly patchwork, but fine appliqué work is also done. Modernization has weakened this custom in Tahiti, the most westernized of the Society Islands. Many women now purchase receiving blankets or make coverlets of lightweight *pareu* cloth and stitch on a border by machine. Pareu cloth is a bold cotton print, usually depicting island flora and made in contrasting colors. Most typically a straight white border and backing is sewn on. The customary pieced tifaifai for infants is now made most often by the families who adhere to the old traditions and on the islands far from the fast pace of westernized Tahiti. The crib tifaifai are made mostly by old women and are scaled-down versions of larger designs. In the islands of Rurutu and Rarotonga, intricate patchwork is made for babies and children. This kind of piecework may include the names (sometimes up to ten) of the newborn child along the borders.

It is not only beginnings that are commemorated with tifaifai. Death and funeral rites are occasions for the use of prized quilts. In Tahiti, coffins are sometimes covered with tifaifai prior to burial, as a pall. This custom, now rarely followed, derives from the old method of wrapping the dead in tapa and mats. The islands that continue to use tifaifai most traditionally in this way are Rurutu and Rarotonga. As an expression of grief and esteem for the dead, only the finest and most treasured tifaifai are used to wrap the body of the loved one. In many cases the casket is covered with tifaifai and the newly-dug grave is lined with the quilts, which are provided by friends and the immediate family. In Rurutu, tifaifai are used in conjunction with fine mats to line graves and wrap caskets.

Any time of national or cultural pride is also a time for tifaifai to be displayed. An example is the annual festival that centers around French Bastille Day observances, the *Heiva i Tahiti*, or Tahiti's festival. Colorful parade floats often have tifaifai draped among the flowers and palm fronds as decorations. It is during an occasion like this that the Tahitian tiputa may be seen. The tiputa is a long poncho-style garment, that was once made of tapa, but is now made of brightly appliquéd cloth. Appliqué was never used for clothing in Tahiti, except for the tiputa. Tiputa patterns are always representational, depicting things like birds, palm trees, flowers, or even *ti'i*, the small statues that were part of the pre-Christian religion. Today the tiputa is worn for only the most important occasions and is an expression of Tahitian pride.

Other holidays that call for the use of tifaifai are Christmas and New Year's. Late-night church services are followed the next day by friends and family calling from house to house. The Tahitian tradition is one of hospitality. On such occasions the best tifaifai are displayed in the home. Among very traditional families, couches, beds, and even walls may be draped with tifaifai to provide a pleasant atmosphere for callers. Refreshments are offered and visitors are sometimes sprinkled with cooling cologne as they enter each home. In close-knit communities families decorate their homes with tifaifai on any Sunday to receive visitors with style.

On the less public level, Tahitians regard tifaifai as special gifts. Many island pastors have collections of tifaifai given to them by their congregations as an expression of love and respect. "Way back, tifaifai were made in the home for our pastors," said one artisan with close ties to the church. "Later on, when there were more churches, women got together in the church buildings to make them. Today, if one pastor leaves for another church or another island, we make all new tifaifai to give to the new pastor and his wife." Often, the recipient of a tifaifai is wrapped in it, a custom that goes back to pre-

A Rarotongan woman proudly displays her patchwork "tivaevae." The quilt on the right is her own work; that on the left is by her mother.

Christian times when sacred relics or kings were ceremonially wrapped in yards of tapa. In this historical context, the gift of a tifaifai is truly a gift of love. Wrapping the quilt around someone wraps him in the affection and approval of those who give it. It is a high honor, indeed.

Another way that Tahitians express their high regard for tifaifai is the quilt exhibition and competition. A gathering of quilts and artisans is a chance to examine the work of others, to learn new ideas and designs, and it is an opportunity to show off and admire the fine quilts that are usually kept hidden away at home. One of the first exhibitions held in Tahiti dates back to 1888. It was held during an industrial and agricultural show in what was then the small village of Papeete.

Today, the biggest quilt exhibition is held just outside Tahiti's capital city of Papeete, where a temporary village is built. This is a village of artisans. Corrugated iron roofs and plywood walls and floors are transformed overnight into a dazzling display of island arts and crafts. Men and women from nearly one hundred craft associations and the five archipelagoes of French Polynesia gather in this village to exhibit and to sell their work. Among the items sold are shellwork, wood carvings, delicate hats of bleached palm, hand-painted pareus, and dresses. But the heart of this village is tifaifai.

During the year, the *mama ruau*, as the craftswomen are known, prepare their tifaifai for the three weeks of exhibition. Most of the tifaifai are for sale, though some, made by beloved mothers and grandmothers, are only for display. Tifaifai are sold in two forms, finished and unfinished. Finished tifaifai are either patchwork, or more often, appliqué. They are cut, basted, and sewn with nearly invisible stitches and are ready for use. Unfinished appliqué tifaifai are cut and basted, and the appliqué stitches are left to the buyer. Prices for unfinished quilts currently average $150 in U.S. currency. Finished tifaifai range from $300 to $1,000 depending on the quality of the work or the originality of the design.

For many artisans, revenues from tifaifai sales can mean a significant portion of the year's income. The government office for traditional artisans has been a strong supporter of the exhibitions, providing funding, helping to procure materials, and offering encouragement and incentives. Because of this support, the art of traditional tifaifai remains strong and in the public eye. Exhibitions are not limited to Tahiti, but have also been put on in France and the United States.

Prior to the 1960s, tifaifai were not for sale in Tahiti. They were only for the Tahitian people or were sometimes given away to an interested visitor. The quilts were first sold in the early 1960s when unprecedented numbers of tourists and French citizens came to the islands. Initially, sales were made from the home, as private commissions. Public sales were first limited to church projects to fund religious study for pastors. But with the escalating numbers of visitors, artisans realized that the tifaifai was in demand and craft associations were born.

There is high unemployment in Tahiti. Older women who are unable to compete in the job market and young high school graduates have turned to the tifaifai to earn a living. Even working women sometimes supplement their incomes by selling tifaifai. An increasingly common sight in Tahiti and the neighboring islands is the thatch-roofed roadside stand, which shelters a foot-powered sewing machine and a woman selling both handmade and machine-made tifaifai to passing tourists. The most frequent buyer of tifaifai, however, is not the tourist but the Polynesian woman. Local women in their twenties and thirties buy them because their work-a-day lifestyles don't allow time for tifaifai making. There is a generation of young women on the main island of Tahiti that has never learned the techniques. Yet tifaifai are highly esteemed and desired as gifts and decoration for the home by these busy young women.

One artisan from Rarotonga moved to Tahiti and decided to stay: "It's better here. You can make money with tifaifai and other crafts. When I lived in Rarotonga, I grew tomatoes for markets in New Zealand. Sometimes I had to wait three months to get the money for my tomatoes. Now, I get paid for my tifaifai right away." Some artisans contract with other young women from their home islands, who come to Tahiti as apprentices and receive a portion of the profits. When the novices have become proficient they go on to earn their own money.

Most artisans are proficient in all stages of tifaifai production. However, there are a number of women who express an inability to design new patterns or to draw them competently. In any group of artisans, there may be one who is designated and recognized by all as a designer. This person has greater artistic skill and can come up with new patterns, variations on old patterns, or can patiently draw complex designs. As a rule, tifaifai making is a female pursuit, but in some cases the designer is a man. In the old Polynesian tradition, some men are brought up to excel in the skills and the work usually performed by women. This is not a sexually-oriented role, but rather a task-oriented role. A number of men are accomplished in all areas of tifaifai manufacture and are recognized as designers and artists.

For the artisan working without the help of a designer, patterns are first worked out on paper. Large sheets of paper in the dimensions of the quilt are taped together to devise a pleasing design. The paper is folded into fourths, one-quarter of the quilt design is drawn on, and then cut out snowflake style to view the final product. If the design is a good one, it is transferred to the cloth and recorded on a four-foot-wide roll of tracing paper. Nearly every tifaifai artisan has a treasured roll of tracing paper filled with tifaifai patterns which can be transferred to cloth again and again.

Transferring a pattern to cloth.
Three layers are visible: the cloth,
the carbon paper, and the paper
with the design. The artisans trace
over the design with pencil. The
pattern created is one quarter of the
total quilt design.

Two artisans cut out the design from fabric that is folded
into fourths. Men also participate in tifaifai making.

When the artisans gather together in the craft village, they begin and end each working day with hymns and a prayer, in keeping with the missionary origins of tifaifai. During the three weeks of the exhibition, the artisans enter into good-natured competitions for the best Polynesian dance routines, the best traditional songs, and the best tifaifai.

On the day of the tifaifai competition, representatives from all craft associations team up to construct quilts on the spot. The best tifaifai qualifies for a cash prize of several hundred dollars, and although this is serious business, the mood is light and the air of competition is almost absent. The women first gather for a song, then they rush to their tables to begin working.

The tables are a uniform size, four feet by eight feet, to accommodate the size of the tifaifai. There are two sheets of fabric of exactly the same size. One is the base fabric which is set aside, the other is the applied top. This piece is typically folded the long way, bringing the eight-foot dimensions together in half, then folding the cloth in half again. The resulting size is approximately three-and-a-half feet by four feet, with the free edges kept together. There is a double folded edge and a single folded edge. The single fold is the central axis of the finished quilt.

Wide sheets of blue carbon paper are then laid on the folded cloth. From a long roll of tracing paper, the chosen design is laid over the carbon and the design is transferred to the cloth. When a scalloped border is incorporated into the design, it is drawn along the free edges of the folded cloth and is the first part of the design to be cut. Several women work together, quickly cutting out the intricate curves and swirls of the pattern. During this frenzied activity, a local band plays Polynesian favorites and a particularly lively tune often sets a grandmother to dancing in hip-shaking Tahitian style.

When the design has been cut out, it is set aside and the base fabric is opened. The eight-foot edge of the table is lined up exactly with the eight-foot edge of the base fabric. The material is then thumbtacked along the table's edge in six- to eight-inch intervals to secure it. Additional tacks are placed along the two short sides of the table. The excess fabric that hangs over the other side of the table is folded up and over and tacked.

The cutout pattern is laid on the base fabric and opened in half, like the pages of a book. The central creases are matched with the creases of the base cloth. The cutout is then opened the rest of the way, very slowly, peeling back the rest of the pattern and tacking the matched creases as they are revealed. The exact center of the pattern is kept on the table. The rest of the pattern is draped over the end of the table, folded up and over and tacked down as before.

All the women then begin basting. They start in the center of the design, concentrating most of the stitches there. Every cut edge is basted down, no matter how tiny. Unexpectedly, a green grasshopper lands on a tifaifai under construction. The women reluctantly slow their pace, making room for it and working around the insect as it walks around the cloth. Grasshoppers are good luck and its landing on the tifaifai is encouraging. (As it turned out, the women of this association did not win this particular competition. But they did win the biggest tifaifai competition of the exhibition and won an even bigger prize.)

Finally, when all are finished, the tifaifai are judged on quality of workmanship, design, color, and speed. The tiny appliqué stitches are done at a later time. The motifs and colors and styles vary from table to table. Some are made in traditional appliqué style, some in reverse appliqué, and some in free-form style without templates or pattern guides of any kind. Prizes are awarded and everyone wins something. And, as they say, a good time is had by all.

A husband and wife are wrapped in a tifaifai in the traditional way. This couple is being honored for its dedication and hard work in making the craft village a success.

This rich floral motif is a fine example of appliqué work in the Rarotongan tradition. Multicolored floral cutouts are set against a dark background, creating strong contrast and a jewel-like effect. Quilts of this type are typically embroidered after appliqué is completed. In this quilt, all edges are embroidered and the flowers and leaves are further defined with embroidery floss in colors of pink, grey, blue, white, red, and deep purple. The patchwork quilt to the left is Pa'aro, a popular pieced design made in strong primary colors. *Made by Teupoo Rangimakea, Fare Maohi Association.*

3.

Design: A Polynesian Perspective

The evolution of the art of quilting during the past two hundred years or so in Tahiti has resulted in several types of quilts being made today. Contemporary tifaifai fall into four basic categories: patchwork, floral appliqué made in the snowflake style, "freestyle" appliqué designs, and Rarotongan-style floral appliqués.

It is in the area of color where the evolution of a Tahitian style is most noticeable. A survey of quilts, both past and present, reveals three distinct palettes: a somber, earth-toned group; quilts of two strong primary colors or the use of one such brilliant color with white; and multi-colored compositions. The oldest group of colors are the muted earth tones. These were originally produced through the use of vegetable dyes, and were used to decorate tapa. Similar colors are used today to recreate this very old look. Only slightly less traditional and historical is the two- or one- primary-color scheme. The colors usually found together or used singly with white are red, blue, or green. Imported commercial fabric in these striking hues became available in Tahiti early in the nineteenth century and gradually increased in use. A majority of the tifaifai made today continue to be of this coloration.

At the same time, other quilt artists are choosing to reflect in their work the uninhibited world of color that is Tahitian. Four, six, and eight colors are used in many of their patterns, most of them in appliqué. This surge of interest in color is a result of more than environmental conditioning. Other factors are an abundance of appealing brightly-colored fabrics in the shops, a general easing of traditional ways within society, and the influence of Rarotongan-style floral appliqué. Some women consider tifaifai of the Rarotongan type more beautiful than traditional Tahitian designs, and they feel more freedom of expression is possible by using numerous colors in one motif. Of course the addition of many colors means that the traditional design structure must change to accomodate those colors. Therefore, traditional Tahitian quilters consider multi-color appliqué patterns inharmonious.

The colors and composition of tifaifai have influenced artists of a different sort. Henri Matisse, the French post-impressionist painter, spent three months in Tahiti during 1930. During a period of creative stagnation, he went there looking for the quality of light and color that had inspired Paul Gauguin, an artist Matisse admired. Matisse reportedly did no painting while there, but sketched extensively, drawing ideas from the voluptuous Tahitian environment. He later became widely known for his brightly colored paper cutouts, which he first created in 1931. By his own admission, some of his later work was based on his experience in Tahiti. Works such as *Polynesia: the Sea, Polynesia: the Sky, The Lagoon,* and *Memories of Oceania,* are those most recognized for Tahitian motifs. However, what has not been recognized about these works is that they are based on tifaifai construction and design. The border work, bold shapes closely resemble tifaifai made in the appliqué style. Matisse's *Polynesia: the Sea* has been made into a tapestry, measuring approximately six feet by ten feet, and when it is viewed as a textile, rather than as a paper cutout, the resemblance to tifaifai is inescapable. The tapestry includes a straight-edge border found on many tifaifai.

In Tahiti, one result of the evolution in tifaifai design is the decline of skill in piecework or patchwork, the *tifaifai pu.* Along with this has come a drop in patchwork popularity. One artisan who still makes the old patchwork patterns says, "They don't like them anymore. They just like big appliqué, cut it out and slap it on." Many of the older women who were proficient in tifaifai pu have passed away. Those who remain and seek to teach younger women find that the young are not interested in learning. Occasionally an extraordinary example of tifaifai pu will surface at an exhibition or during a special occasion. In some cases these were made by mothers or grandmothers. In other instances the quilts may have come from another island or were made by a woman who moved to Tahiti and brought patchwork skills with her. Some artists who sell tifaifai are making small amounts of patchwork, but pattern pieces are bigger than they once were and are often machine-stitched.

The Tahitian patchwork that is most admired in the islands and is most representative of regional styles and Polynesian invention is the pieced mosaic. Tiny squares, one inch or smaller, are pieced to form pictures or complicated designs. Most mosaic designs are floral, such as *Orchide,* illustrated and diagrammed on pp. 80-85. Early mosaics were made in two colors, red and white. Contemporary examples of these quilts, when found, are made with numerous colors and reflect the colors of the chosen flowers in the motif.

Traditional patch patterns from the 1800s are still made by some women. Most of these patterns are similar to patchwork patterns made in the West. Among them is the island version of Barn Raising or Log Cabin, known locally as *Patu,* or gathering (see p. 33). Another frequently made pattern is a variation of Sunshine and Shadow, commonly known by the generic name, tifaifai pu, (see p. 72). Both of these patterns are believed to have originated with English missionaries.

Other traditional patchwork patterns that resemble their Western counterparts include Honeycomb, Sawtooth, and Bear's Paw. Bear's Paw motifs are known as *Rimarima,* or touching hands, and are made primarily in red and white. *Pa'aro,* a version of Drunkard's Path or Robbing Peter to Pay Paul, is widely made and artisans choose strong primary colors for these quilts. The Star of Bethlehem pattern is known by many Tahitian artisans. It is made of multicolored scraps, the numbers of points vary widely, and it is usually applied to a large sheet of white cloth. Some women see this pattern as a sun, but the common name is *fetia* or star. Some of these quilts, although widely made and exhibited, are not represented here with photographs. There is a longstanding tradition of secrecy among Polynesians regarding their tifaifai designs. Some of the quilters who adhere to this tradition would not allow their quilts to be photographed. However, these patterns are so commonly made that they must be included in any discussion of Tahitian patchwork.

Most patchwork executed today is found in pillow slips called *vehiturua,* or pillow in. Because they are less time-consuming to make, these are usually hand-pieced. Much daily living is conducted on the floor and pillows serve a practical purpose as well as a decorative one. Pillows are often made to form complete sets with tifaifai of the same motif. One of the most typical pillow motifs is the star or half-star pillow called *taratara* in reference to the multicolored patches in the pattern.

Star pillows are found in many Tahitian homes. The half-star design Taratara is one of the most popular and is made in rose pink, lime green, white, navy blue, yellow, and red. After hand-piecing, the star design is attached to a solid color backing and then stuffed. *Made by Association Artisanale Mato Ura Ura-Paea.*

Lili is an example of the tifaifai pu mosaic style. Quilts of this type were once commonplace in Tahiti but are fast disappearing. Similar tifaifai pu are made in several islands of eastern Polynesia. This one originated in Rurutu, the Austral Islands. Pieced quilts of this type are typically made by dividing the pattern into eight triangular sections which are distributed to several women for piecing. The patches for each section are organized on long strings in the proper order for joining. There are irregularities in the placement of some of the pattern pieces, probably due to an error in stringing the colors together. The patches on this tifaifai pu are less than one inch square. *Courtesy of Areratai Tamarii Association, Rurutu.*

Patterned fabrics were commonly used in the older forms of tifaifai pu. These patches are part of a quilt made between 1907-1911. The scraps are hand-pieced and made from Indonesian batik, the old style pareu cloth once sold in Tahiti. The colors have faded, but include brown, white, blue, pale green, pink, and red.

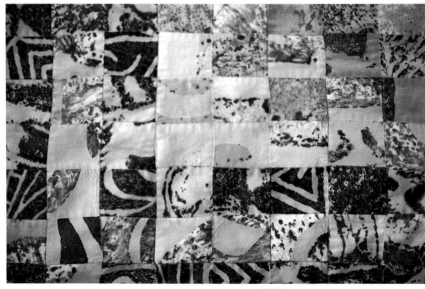

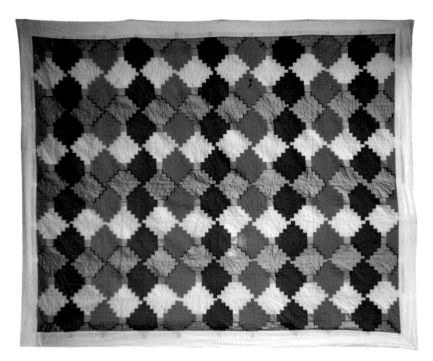

Patu is an old patch pattern thought to go back to the earliest days of Tahitian quilting. This quilt resembles Log Cabin and Barn Raising patterns made in the West. The name *patu* refers to gathering and says more about the technique than the motif, as the design is made with cotton strips. Horizontal rows of yellow and green appear to be intersected with vertical rows of orange and red. The quilt is framed with a white border. *Made by Taaria Walker, Tiare Porea Association.*

Identified by its maker only as Pu, this pattern dates back to the mid- to late 1800s. The radiating diamonds are assembled by joining disproportionate pieces into blocks. (These same blocks are used to make Pa'aro.) Tahitian artisans of the 1800s made many variations of this pattern. Some wood carvings found on tapa beaters and ceremonial objects had similar designs and this may account for the pattern's popularity. The quilt is made in contrasting colors of robin's egg blue and orange, and is backed and bordered with pale green. *Made by Marguerite Tapatoa, Tiare Opuhi Association, Papeari.*

Under the general heading of appliquéd tifaifai, there are three basic styles. The most predominant is the tifaifai *pa'oti,* which refers to cutting—the traditional snowflake form (discussed on this page), and the freestyle and Rarotongan floral style (discussed on p. 44). Scissor-cutting from folded cloth in the snowflake method is the backbone of Tahitian quilting. The methods of construction are always the same; the fabric is folded into fourths and the design is cut from the folded cloth. Colors are usually limited to two. Reverse appliqués are made in the same manner. Chosen colors contrast sharply. Flatness rather than three-dimensionality is considered most beautiful.

There are many places in the world where children have taken a sheet of paper, folded it, and from it cut a design, a "snowflake." The Tahitian quilter has taken this simple skill and turned it into a sophisticated textile art. Tahitian appliquéd tifaifai are distinctive, even from the appliqué work done by neighboring islanders. Snowflake appliqué designs are taken from nature and are almost always representational—patterns are never simply snowflakes or randomly designed cutouts. Patterns such as *Uru,* (breadfruit) *Opuhi, Pua,* and *Tiare* (three flowers) are distinctly Polynesian in flavor and are without Western counterparts.

The earliest Tahitian appliqué quilts were composed of small cutouts applied to blocks or placed against a larger sheet of cloth. Even laboriously pieced designs were sometimes applied to a base fabric. Today's appliqué work, however, is larger than life. The transformation of small, frugal cutouts to the huge bed-sized designs can only be attributed to Polynesian invention and exuberance. The unrestrained size of the designs results from the extraordinary size of island flora.

Fans and French eagles are very old motifs. This contemporary quilt was done in the style of the royal patterns once made by the Tahitian *arii*. Fans were symbols of royalty in many of the islands, while the eagles were probably incorporated into tifaifai patterns after the arrival of the French in the 1840s. The blue and white color combination is not as traditional as red and white, but it is a hallmark of the period. The complex double border is cut from one piece and resembles fleurs-de-lis, another indication this Tahirihiri pattern may have been influenced by French colonists. *Made by Naita, Papeiha Nui Association, Hitiaa.*

This close-up look at a variation of the Tahirhiri pattern of fans and French eagles reveals the expertise of Tahitian artisans. Careful basting and nimble fingers produced nearly-invisible appliqué stitches. Blue thread was used to appliqué the blue design to the white backing. Tahitians do not use hoops or frames when they appliqué; the whole quilt is bundled on the lap and sewn one tiny bit at a time.

In this detail of the Meherio pattern (see opposite page), note that the turned-back edges of the white cloth are very thin. Most artisans leave a ½ " allowance to turn under. To keep the intricate curves of this pattern flat, a smaller allowance was used. Overcast stitches were used to attach the white design to the navy blue backing.

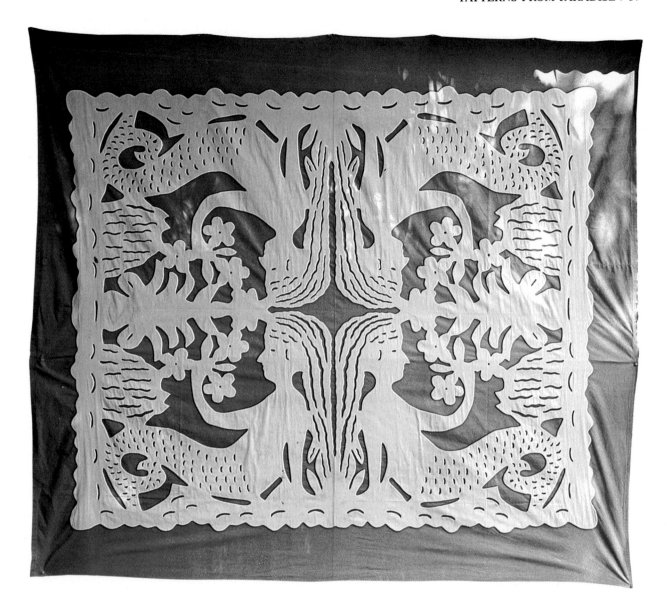

On certain nights, when there is no wind and the moon is reflected in the water, rendering a still and shiny surface, Tahitian legends say you may see the *meherio,* the mermaids. The stories are numerous, but all agree the mermaids are beautiful to behold and intend no harm. Island children who were brought up with these stories keep the legends alive in the tifaifai they create as adults. The mermaid motif is an unusual quilt subject because it is one of the few designs based on something other than real objects. And interestingly, this treatment of mermaids is presented more realistically than most; a typical mermaid quilt pattern is far more stylized and difficult to visualize.

This is a difficult pattern to cut and to sew. Many small scales on the mermaid's tail require an expert touch. The quilter used very fine overcast stitches to keep the lines of the hair and the scales thin and controlled. *Made by Teri Collet, Pupu Rima I Manava Association, Outumaoro.*

What could be more fitting than a pattern of pineapples? The fruit is an island favorite. Tahitian pineapples *(painapo)* are allowed to ripen on the plant and have a sweetness and aroma hard to resist. Pineapples were once grown almost exclusively on large plantations as a cash crop. Now they are grown in the home garden. Surplus is sold at roadside stands.

Although the color combination seems impulsive, the design picks up and intensifies the colors of the pineapple rind. This is a dense pattern that fills up the space of the quilt in keeping with the standards of good tifaifai design. Pineapple motifs have become commonplace, but this quilter added her own touch with the extra scalloping on both sides of the quilt. The orange framing border appears to be a separately cut piece, but it is the base fabric that creates the impression of a border. Four of the pineapples have a thin, misshapen look; most of the old Painapo designs were distorted in this way. *Made by Elise Poimata, Te Hotu O Te Fenua Association, Mahina.*

Good tifaifai design is exemplified in this pattern of flowers and vines—Tiare with Vines. The colors are bright and stand out sharply against each other. Even though the applied top consists of narrow strips of fabric, the pattern is bold. There is a minimum of empty space and the white and pink are evenly proportioned.

The seamstress achieved a fine sense of balance by anchoring the light and airy pattern with a heavier scalloped border. To cut this pattern, the quilter removed sections of the pink material. The tifaifai required extra care in centering and basting and was appliquéd with very tiny overcast stitches. The quilt has a somewhat different look than most of the floral appliqués as it was made by an artisan from the Tuamotu Islands. The Tuamotu islanders are next-door neighbors to Tahitians, but their tifaifai have a different flavor, both in appliqué and patchwork. *Made by Mariana Tokorahi, Tiare Kahaia Association, Tuamotus.*

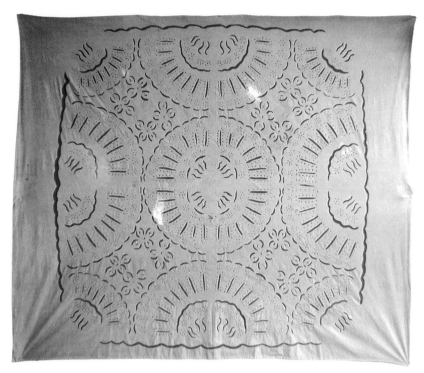

This antique quilt exhibits very early appliqué techniques in the Tahirihiri style. The Chinese fan motif dates back to the mid-1800s. The pattern is made by using reverse appliqué techniques. The brown fabric on top is cut to allow the maroon fabric underneath to form the design. Within the fans are dozens of tiny circles, cut with diameters between $\frac{1}{8}''$ and $\frac{1}{4}''$. The owners of this tifaifai were unsure of its age but all agreed it is "very old." This is an example of the kind of work done by former generations of Tahitian women. *Made by Diana Huuti, Vahine Ma Pore Association, Marquesas.*

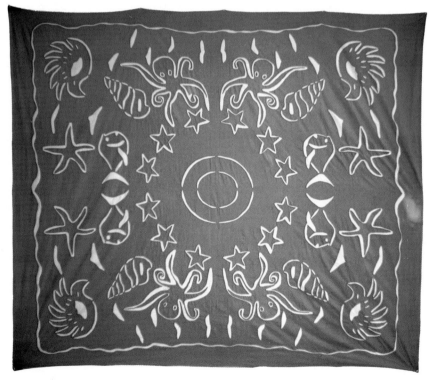

Te Miti is the Tahitian name for the sea and this pattern. The ocean, reefs, and lagoons surrounding the islands have naturally been a strong influence on the art of the Tahitian people. This is a contemporary pattern. The treatment of the motif is very original and the artisan displays a light and humorous touch. The quilt is made using reverse appliqué techniques. The yellow base fabric shows through the red fabric on top. The contrasting colors of yellow and red are traditional (see Pūpū on p. 108) and bring this tifaifai into the mainstream of Tahitian quilting. Some of the shapes, like the starfish, are cut out and lifted from the design, then replaced and appliquéd. *Made by Ruth Pihatarioe, Hapaiano Association, Papenoo.*

The Pua design is based on a trumpet-shaped flower of the same name and is one of the most popular subjects for appliquéd tifaifai. The three concentric circles are connected; they are formed by cutting the pattern from folded cloth. The choice of white against navy blue is unusual for the Pua motif; most floral appliqués adhere to the natural colors of the flower they depict. The border is also unusual. The outside edge of the top fabric has been left as it was cut, with only a thin edge of blue defining the outermost flowers. *Made by Tufaana Mohi, Papeiha Nui Association, Hitiaa.*

One of the best loved Tahitian flowers is the *tipani,* also known as frangipani or plumeria. Pink, white, and yellow varieties grow just about everywhere on twisted little trees that look like hedges gone mad. Tipani has a fresh and pleasing fragrance and is a favorite decoration for *heis*—wreaths of flowers worn on the head.

The startling purple and yellow used in Tipani is a fine example of how Tahitian artisans use color. The yellow represents the yellow tipani flower; the purple gives the pattern its contrast. Open flowers and immature buds are arranged to give the design a light, airy look, an effect picked up by the scalloped inner border, which is also made lighter by the placement of tiny floral shapes within the scalloping. The design is kept small, in the old appliqué style. *Made by Jeanne, Bougainville Association.*

Vines are often overlooked in favor of more colorful tropical flora. But in Tahiti, vines snake up the coconut trees, the sides of mountains, and the back yards of houses. Most Tahitian vines have very large leaves, true to the growth patterns of the tropics, but the leaves on this tifaifai are small by island standards, and resemble ivy. The size of the leaves, the choice of coral and brown earth tones, and the small design panel placed without a border indicate that this pattern is an old one. The wide margin serves as a border and recalls the time when fabric was scarce and borders were often omitted. *Made by Paia Turu, Vahine Tahaa Association, Tahaa.*

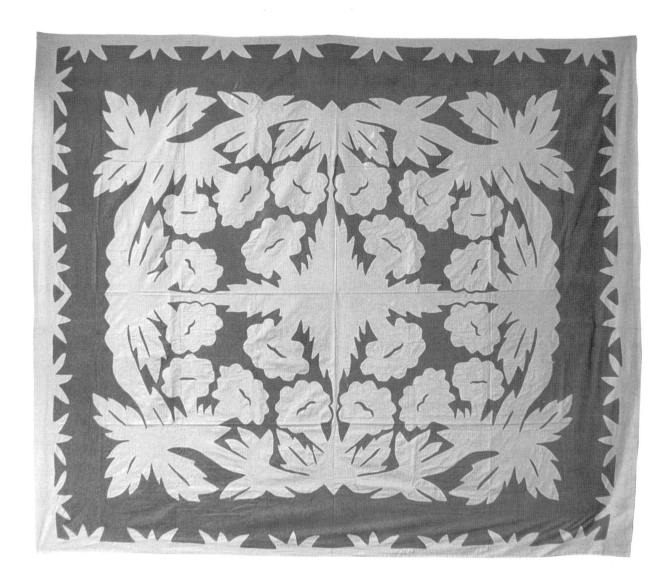

The *pua* is a delicate trumpet-shaped flower with a sweet scent that is native to the Society Islands. Tahitian legends say that the flowering plant was sent to Tahiti by Tane, an ancient god, as a gift to the island people. Groves of pua trees are scattered throughout the mountains and valleys of Tahiti and, long ago, these groves were considered sacred.

The true colors of the flowers are soft shades of cream, white, and yellow. The artisan has chosen cream and cognac to reflect authentic shades, but she has kept the contrast sharp and within the rules of tifaifai design. This is a classic Pua pattern, circular and symmetrical. *Made by Terii, Papeiha Nui Association, Hitiaa.*

The two remaining and most colorful of the three appliqué quilt styles are the freestyle and the Rarotongan floral. The large Rarotongan floral appliqué quilts exhibit the most indulgent use of color. Called *tivaevae* by the women of the Cook Islands, who originated them, these quilts consist of huge floral patterns averaging eighteen to twenty-four inches across. These are appliquéd to a solid backing using only enough color repetition to create symmetry. The appliqués are further embellished with embroidery floss, which may include several colors as well. The embroidery is heavy and thick, adding texture to these lush and colorful quilts.

More common to Tahitian quilting than the Rarotongan floral is the freestyle quilt. (Tahitians have no special name for this type, but refer to it only as tifaifai appliqué.) Breaking with the traditional snowflake form (tifaifai pa'oti), these artists create bold and colorful scenes of island life. The representational designs include motifs which have been avoided in other types of appliqué, such as animals and people. The freestyle appliqués produced today are recent innovations on earlier appliqué forms in which small representative designs are scattered on white sheeting, often in random fashion. The quilters use templates or freely cut pattern pieces to form their picture quilts. Contemporary quilts may have patterned fabric incorporated into the design. No limits are placed on the number of colors used and five to ten colors on one quilt are not unusual. The colors are kept true to nature, however: a lagoon is blue, a palm tree is green, and an hibiscus flower, red.

Here is a close-up view of the central medallion of the Tiare Opuhi motif (see p. 45). The design is one of long spikes of red ginger and the green sword-like leaves that surround the flowers. The medallion is appliquéd to a white background with a tiny slipstitch. Leaves are cut from folded cloth; flowers are cut from templates. Medallions such as this are unusual in Tahitian appliqué and are thought to have originated with British missionaries. This medallion is about two feet tall.

This is an excellent tifaifai depicting a familiar flower, the *tiare opuhi*. The opuhi is a type of ginger that produces dark red or deep pink waxy flowers. The flower spikes grow up to a foot-and-a-half tall on mature plants and are surrounded by large sword-like leaves. The plant was once an important source of vegetable dye.

The usual treatment of Tiare Opuhi motifs includes a central wreath of green leaves with the flowers radiating out like spokes on a wheel. The flowers usually alternate pink with red. This artisan has remodeled the more familiar pattern and created two concentric circles. One is the traditional green wreath, which is studded with opuhi buds; the second circle is constructed of mature flowers and leaves.

Two techniques are used to make this quilt: templates and cutouts from folded cloth. Opuhi flowers, buds, and leaves are made with templates; the pieces are not cut singly, but in fours. The inner wreath of leaves is cut from folded cloth, snowflake style. Green edging frames the tifaifai. *Made by Marguerite Tapatoa, Tiare Opuhi Association, Papeari.*

An unidentified pattern of flowers, called here Tiare, is typical of the multicolored designs from the Rarotongan or Cook Islands that have become very popular in Tahiti. The use of so many colors is causing some concern among traditional artisans, but the effect is striking. The scalloped border is cut from folded cloth in the usual manner. The same color is picked up in two of the center rose-colored flowers, a placement which helps to pull the design together.

After the flowers and border are hand-appliquéd, machine-made zigzag stitching is used to outline the border and the green leaves. White threads add more definition. The use of the sewing machine in appliqué work is increasing but quilts made in this manner are considered less valuable by many women. *Made by Atea Poroi, Tiare Vaiete Association.*

The Tahitian people have a strong love for their islands. Quilters in the classic Tahitian appliqué tradition take one element from nature and base a design on it. Freestyle quilts are very different. The quilter has communicated a love of the land with a tableau, a whole slice of rural Tahitian life rather than a single element. The pattern pieces are big and bold and represent things both beautiful and important to islanders. The herons that feed in shallow lagoons were once considered sacred. The *mei'a,* one of many types of bananas grown on the islands, and the traditional way of gathering them are depicted here. The message is one of an abundant and generous land. *Courtesy of Tamatea Association.*

Although most quiltmakers prefer complex designs, this simple Fe'i pattern is popular because it represents another species of native Tahitian banana. The fe'i is loved as much for its origin as its fruit. Tahitian men still hike into the mountains to gather fe'i and bring them down lashed to bamboo poles carried across the shoulders. Fe'i is more than food; it is a part of life.

Templates are used to cut the four banana plants and the four bunches of fe'i. Green fabric has been placed beneath the bananas to provide contrast at the turned-back edges. *Made by Thelena Bourguois, Maha Te Aho Association, Hitiaa.*

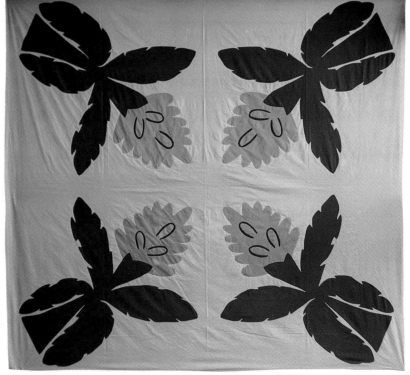

4.   A Gallery of Tahitian Designs

W hen making tifaifai, Tahitian quiltmakers adhere to a few basic principles. The following information, along with the specific instructions for each quilt, will help every quilter to re-create the designs successfully.

For an appliquéd quilt, two sheets of fabric of exactly the same size are needed (unless instructions specify a different size). The standard quilt measures 8' × 7'. Wide cotton sheets are best (they may have to be ordered) or bedsheets in the full flat size can be used. My feeling is that bedsheets are too flimsy for the quilts. Another alternative is to buy fabric by the yard and sew the widths together to create a large surface. Tahitians feel that only cotton cloth should be used. Use only cotton with cotton. A cotton top and poly/cotton bottom may result in pulling of the applied top and the tiny appliqué stitches. Cotton thread should be used with cotton cloth.

A good quality cotton fabric with a high thread count is preferable. The heavier the cotton, the stronger and longer lasting the quilt. Also, heavy cotton fabric is easier to appliqué, particularly in tight corners or tiny cutout edges that are turned under during appliqué. The better the cotton, the less fraying of edges. Cotton fabrics should be pre-shrunk. To insure colorfastness, the finished quilt can be soaked in salt water overnight. Tahitian artisans say that salt water prevents colors from bleeding and they soak tifaifai in the sea for a day or two before washing in cool fresh water.

Before beginning work, both sheets of cloth should be folded into fourths and pressed lightly with an iron. This will help to center accurately the creases of the design. Tahitian quiltmakers attach borders to the base fabric first. The creases of the base fabric and border are carefully matched before stitching. The rest of the design is centered within the border, with carefully matched creases as the guide.

The graphed drawings in this chapter are one quarter of the total quilt design. The graph and its design will have to be enlarged to the average size of 3½' × 4'. (Check the size of the chosen quilt first.) To enlarge the graph take a large sheet of paper and draw the exact number of horizontal and vertical lines as on the pattern graph. Square by square, draw each portion of the pattern. It may help to number the outside squares.

To transfer the design to the folded cloth, use large sheets of dressmaker's carbon, taped together, and place the carbon directly on the cloth. Place the graphed design on top of the carbon. Trace the design with a pen to impress it onto the cloth. Tahitian quiltmakers keep the impression very light, but to be able to follow the design clearly when cut, make sure the impression is clear and sharp. Pin the fabric layers together after the design is transferred.

A piece of plywood, 4' × 8', can be laid on a table and used to position, thumbtack, and pin the pattern. Basting takes place on the table and it can take a couple of days to complete, depending on the complexity of the pattern. The 8' edge of the table corresponds to the average 8' width of the tifaifai. The edges of the cloth are thumbtacked to the table. Position the fabric on the table one half at a time. The exact center of the quilt is always kept on the table and is shifted from one side of the table to the other as basting of each side is finished.

If a quilt with a border is chosen, draw and cut the border along the loose edges of the folded cloth. When the border is cut it opens into one piece. To attach the border, both the base fabric and the border are placed wrong side up. Use a sewing machine to stitch the straight edges (or a running stitch can be used), then turn the border up and over to the right side and baste the edges. Basting is done about ½" from the edge. When basting the main part of the design, begin in the center and work outward. Keep a small pair of scissors handy to notch troublesome curves or angles when appliquéing.

Two patchwork projects are included among the projects—Tifaifai Pu on pp. 72-75 and Orchide, pp. 80-85—and special instructions are given with each.

Te Vahine E Te Miti

Te Vahine e Te Miti means the woman and the sea. This tifaifai was created for a competition of the same name. Several people had a hand in making the quilt; it was designed by a man, sewn by several women, and embroidered by two other women in a true cooperative [effor]t. The design represents the tranquil side of Polynesian life and [its r]eliance upon the sea. Incorporated in the scene are the beautiful [b]asic elements of island life; it is a celebration. This type of idyllic [scen]e is fast disappearing from the island of Tahiti, but still exists [in ne]ighboring islands and other islands of French Polynesia. The [wah]ine is wearing the traditional *pareu,* a simple piece of cloth that [is wra]pped and tied around the body. The outrigger canoe, seen at [the bo]rder, is still used throughout Polynesia.

[A]lthough it depicts a traditional scene, the quilt is non-traditional [in thre]e ways. First, such a freeform pattern is a recent innovation. [Second], the quilter has used eight colors rather than one or two. And [finally], the design is heavily embroidered. Embroidery is used here [to ...]definition to the palm trees, the figure of the woman, the fish, [and ...]flower behind her ear.

[The] border is cut from one whole piece of cloth laid out flat. [The] template pieces of hair, legs, arms, etc., are simple to cut and [... can] be made from a yard of cloth with some leftovers. Although [various c]olors have been used, the fabrics should all be cottons of [similar w]eight to prevent pulling during the appliqué. *Courtesy of [... A]ho Association, Hitiaa.*

51

Dimensions: 6½' × 7½'

Both the top and bottom fabrics should match in size. One yard of cloth will be needed for the rock and canoe. The yellow pareu requires about one half yard; the hair, one yard; and the woman's skin, a little over one yard. Always buy a few extra inches to be safe.

To remain true to the pattern, enlarge the border graph to the size of the fabric or draw the border on the cloth freehand. The cloth is not folded. The border is drawn on the open cloth and then cut out.

Attach the border by placing the base fabric and the border wrong side up. Sew the perimeters of the border with machine or running stitch. Turn the border up and over and pin. Do not baste down yet.

Cut the template pieces with ¼" allowance. Arrange on the fabric as shown and baste well. Turn the edges under and appliqué to the base fabric using widely spaced stitches. Embroidery floss has been used to appliqué the edges of the border and to create definition in leaves, palm trees, fish, and other elements. The woman's eye, mouth, fingernails, and the flower behind her ear are all done with embroidery floss. Various stitches are used, including chain stitch and satin stitch.

Graph pattern pieces:
1 square = 1$\frac{5}{16}$"

Up ↑

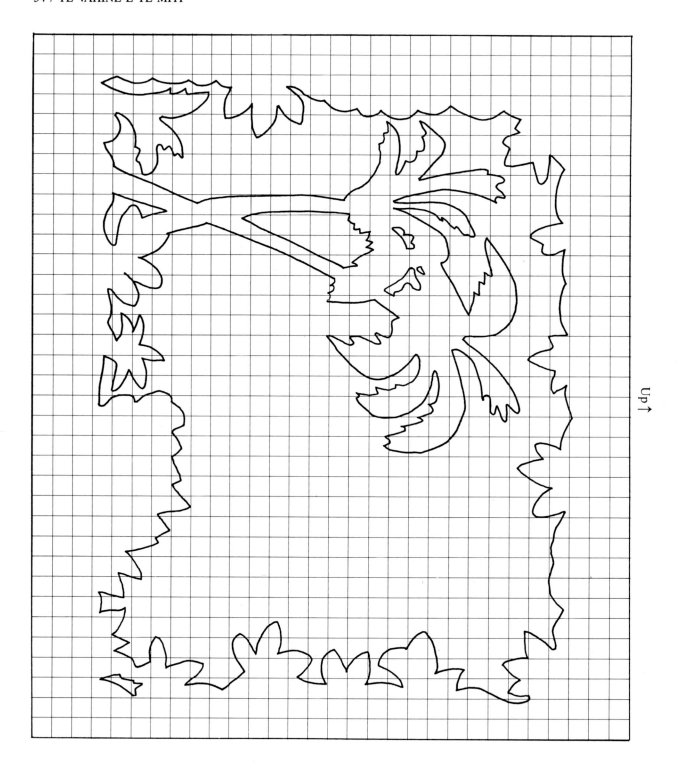

Up↑

Border graph pattern:
1 square = 2⅝″

Complete graph pattern:
1 square = $2\frac{5}{8}''$

Aute

A symbol of the tropics, the single red hibiscus is native to Tahiti. Yellow, pink, coral, and white single varieties, as well as lush doubles, were introduced in the mid-1800s and are now widely cultivated. Early Tahitians planted this flower to mark mountain trails through thick vegetation. Women of Polynesia, both young and old, adorn themselves with the hibiscus flower, known as *tiare aute*. Traditionally, it has been a source of a dye, a plant medicine, and a motif for old-style tapa cloth.

The Aute design is an old and widespread tifaifai motif. Variations of the design seem endless, though the chosen colors are usually limited to red and pink, in keeping with the actual colors of the flower. This particular pattern is composed of four large pattern pieces symmetrically arranged along the border. The scalloped border is cut from folded fabric. Although the cloth is folded into fourths for cutting, close examination reveals that the pieces are not joined together. This design reflects the simplicity of the indigenous red hibiscus, and is a good introductory tifaifai to make. *Made by Roura Tuhiti and Tehei Tuhiti, Association Artisanale, Mato Ura Ura, Paea.*

Dimensions: 8' × 7'

Four large pattern pieces are used to create this elegant hibiscus motif. Because the pieces are not joined, this is an easy pattern to make.

Fold the fabric into fourths: the 8' width is folded in half first, bringing the fabric toward you. Fold in half again, keeping the single fold to the left. Transfer the pattern from the graph to the cloth with carbon paper. Pin all four layers together and cut, leaving a minimum ¼" allowance. The slits in the petals and leaves are picked up between the fingers and cut as a single line. The small circles at the flower stamens are snipped as a small X.

Fix the border to the base fabric, center the creases, and stitch along the straight edges with machine or running stitches. Turn the border up and over, pin the edges, and baste. Arrange the pattern pieces on the backing so they do not touch each other and there is ample room between the design and the border. Baste from the center and work out to the edges. Be sure to baste every cut edge, including the petal slits.

Graph pattern:
1 square = 1⅜″

Uru

Uru is the Tahitian name for breadfruit. It was this fruit Captain Bligh was after in 1788 when he lost his ship, the *Bounty,* in that famous mutiny. Tahitian legends say that breadfruit was born from a father's love for his family. During a severe famine, when there was nothing to eat but red earth, the father appealed to his god for help and then died. His body miraculously turned into a breadfruit tree overnight, providing food for his family and food enough for all ever since. In fact, breadfruit was used to stave off famine. It was buried in underground pits, allowed to ferment, and kept for hard times. Uru originated in the Indo-Malay region and is thought to be among the foodstuffs brought by ancient Polynesians when they settled the islands. The breadfruit tree is a beautiful one, casting deep shade and bearing heavy fruit twice a year.

The Uru motif is most traditionally made in two shades of green or green and white. Breadfruit designs tend to be simple with little embellishment. The frequent absence of borders on these patterns suggests the design is an old one and that the tradition is being upheld. This pattern, an example of pure Polynesian design, having no counterpart in Western quilting, has a graceful and pleasing symmetry and accurately depicts the tree. A simple pattern, Uru is suitable for the novice in appliqué. *Made by Taae Raymonde, Vahine Aumaitai Association.*

Dimensions: 8' × 7'

Uru is one of the easiest tifaifai to make. Two sheets of cloth are necessary and must be of exactly the same size. The pattern is reproduced by enlarging the graph on a large sheet of paper. When the cloth is folded into fourths, the measurement will be 4' × 3½'. The graph should be this same size.

Fold the fabric in fourths, keeping the loose edges together and to the right and in front of you, the folded edges to the left and opposite you. Line up the pattern with the single folded edge on the left. This is the true center of the quilt. Transfer the pattern using carbon paper. Pin all layers together and begin cutting from the outer edges. Leave at least a ¼ " allowance when cutting. Leaf shapes should be cut with a wider allowance.

Open the design in half on the base fabric. Center all creases, eliminate wrinkles, and tack the central creases with thumbtacks. Pin the remaining part of the design. Baste all edges, beginning in the center of the design, placing basting stitches about ½ " from the edge. Appliqué is done with overcast or blind hem stitch. Use cotton thread with cotton cloth.

Graph pattern:
1 square = 1⅜″

Up↑

Roti (A)

The rose or *roti,* is not a native Tahitian flower, but it has caught the imagination of tifaifai artists. Variations of the Roti motif are widely used. Because of the borrowing of patterns between quilters throughout Polynesia, rose patterns show up on islands where the flower has never been cultivated. Roses often appear on wedding tifaifai and such floral patterns are sometimes also used to decorate a house where a wedding feast is held. The Western rose is small, but in this tifaifai each is enlarged to the size of native tropical flora. Bold splashy blossoms, together with sharply contrasting colors, create a strong visual impact.

This tifaifai is constructed using templates. Flowers are not cut out individually, but in Tahitian style, they are cut four at a time from folded cloth. Leaves and buds are cut the same way. The border is cut from the edges of the folded fabric in the typical manner. By keeping the border narrow and by placing three slits at regular intervals in the scalloping, the border does not compete with the roses, but frames them with a light touch. Traditionally, large template designs such as this have been scarce. But they have become more popular in recent years, probably due to the influence of Rarotongan patterns, a style in which large floral designs are common. *Made by Noho Teariki, Te Vahine Noho Paeava Association.*

Dimensions: 8' × 7'

This colorful tifaifai is easy to draw and cut. A template for the flowers can be made or the rose pattern can be transferred to the folded cloth with carbon, and the roses cut four at a time.

The fabric for the roses and the border is folded into fourths. Keep the single folded edge to the left. Transfer the border design, pin the layers together well, and begin by cutting the small slits in the border. Cut the border off, leaving at least ¼ " allowance.

Transfer the rose design to the folded cloth and cut out four at a time. The extra rose will be used to form the four buds. The twenty-eight leaves are cut from green fabric folded into fourths and cut four at a time.

Attach the border to the base fabric by sewing the straight edges. Turn the border up and over to the right side, pin, and baste. Arrange the roses, leaves, and buds as shown. Baste all edges.

Graph border and pattern pieces:
1 square = 1⅜"

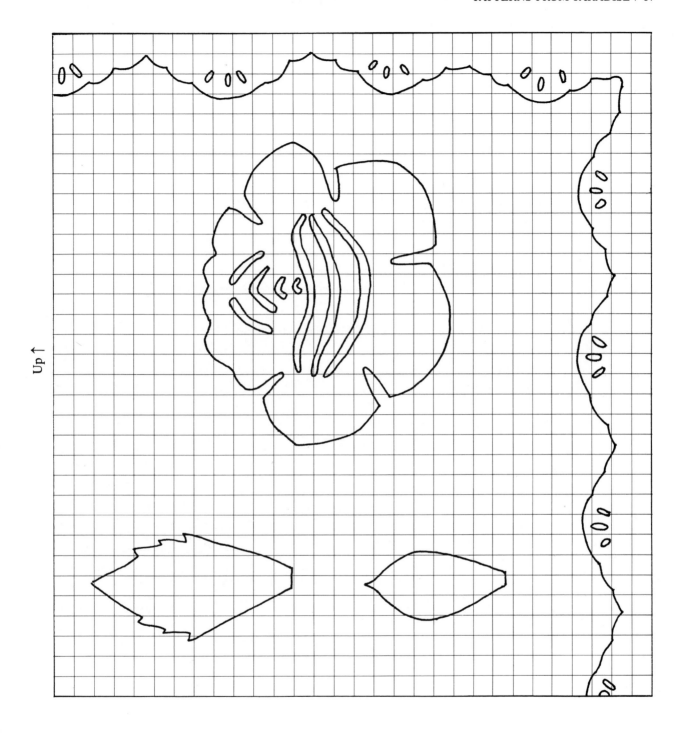

Chou

Chou is a pattern made up of cabbages. Although the vegetable seems an unlikely motif for quilting, the development of this pattern is a reflection of the Tahitian artisan's talent for seeing something in nature (or the marketplace) and setting it down in cloth. The color choices of deep pink and purple reinforce the motif. Elongated leaves, seen in fan palms and similar vegetation around the islands, have been a motif for tifaifai for many years. A pattern with some resemblance to this is *Pua Mahana,* a type of sunflower, whose petals are arranged in similar fashion.

The graceful lines of the appliqué are picked up by the generous use of scalloping in both the inner and outer borders. The concave sides of the outer border result in a rounded look that complements the curving lines of the central design. This tifaifai requires careful basting and precise placement of the top fabric on the exact center of the base fabric. Note how the scalloped edges of the two borders, located at the top and bottom of the tifaifai, correspond exactly. *Made by Myrna Ti-paon, Te Fare Vahine A Tahu Association, Tautira.*

Dimensions: 8' × 7'

It might help to practice cutting this pattern on paper before cutting it in cloth. To do so, tape together large sheets of paper to match the size of the quilt, fold in fourths, and cut it out.

To begin, open the fabric with the 8' dimension placed horizontally. Fold the cloth in half, bringing it toward you. Fold it in half again, keeping the single folded edge to the left. Transfer the pattern from the enlarged graph to the cloth using carbon paper. Pin the fabric layers together and begin cutting the outside border. While cutting the rest of the design, note that there are four narrow areas near the folded edges of the cloth. Do not cut into them or the pattern will separate. Leave ¼" allowance.

When cutting the inner border (which is part of the main design), pinch the fabric up between the fingers and take small snips with the point of the scissors to form the petal shapes. The elongated spaces within the cabbage leaves are cut as simple curving lines.

First attach the outside border to the base fabric. Both are wrong side up. Stitch the straight edges, then turn the border up, over, and baste the edges down. Center the cabbage design on the base fabric and open in half. Center all creases, peel the top of the design back and tack all creases to the table. Pin and baste from the center and work out. Shift the pattern on the table to complete the other half in the same way.

Graph pattern:
1 square = 1⅜"

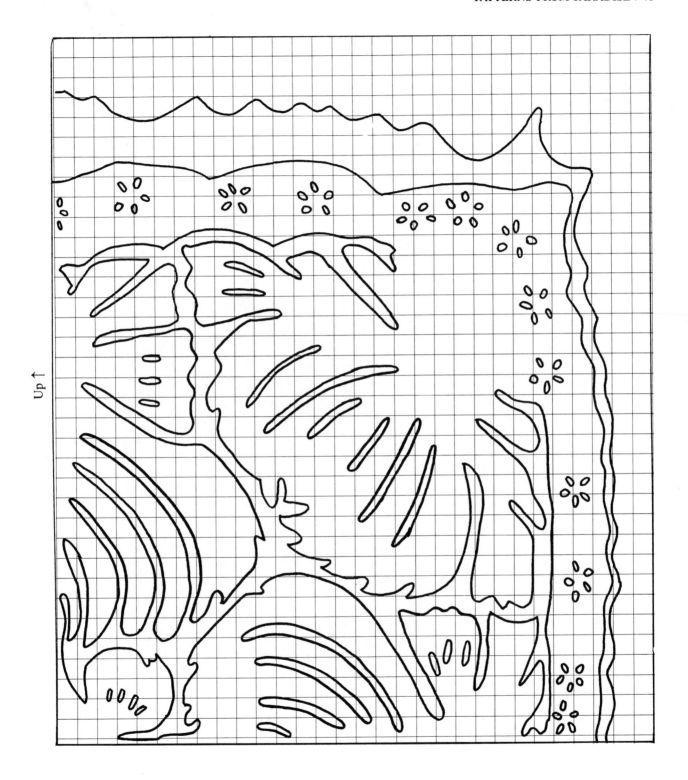

Tifaifai Pu

"This is the real old time tifaifai," says Jeanne, the maker of the crib quilt shown here. Tifaifai Pu is the name given to piecework done with tiny square or rectangular patches. This quilt was faithfully made in the old patch pattern taught by missionary wives. Because fabric was scarce, early quilts of this type were made in fewer colors. Many were executed entirely in red and white. As more fabric became available, the pattern was rendered in a rainbow of colors and the quilt became much larger in size. The pattern resembles the familiar Sunshine and Shadow and Trip Around the World designs of the West. Earlier, when patchwork rather than appliqué was widely done in Tahiti, the pattern was also created with hexagons and lozenges.

The small size of this quilt is similar to the size of original patchwork, about 5¼ ′ square. This size is now reserved for baby tifaifai, first made in anticipation of a birth by relatives of the mother. A woman who didn't have a collection of tifaifai in which to wrap her baby was an unfortunate woman, indeed. Today these infant quilts are disappearing from Tahitian layettes in favor of commercially available blankets and sheets.

Tifaifai Pu begins with a central red square surrounded by four blue squares all turned on the axis. Ten concentric squares are formed by forty rows of repeating colors. Twelve colors are used in this pattern, excluding the central square. The center of the design is twisted, a problem that shows up often in Tahitian patchwork. The quilt top and backing are not joined by any kind of stitching except that used along the border. It might be wise to tack the top and backing together at intervals. *Made by Jeanne, Bougainville Association.*

Dimensions: 5¼' square

The quilt is assembled by making four separate large triangles. Each of the triangles has a zig-zag pattern of tiny squares. Triangles #1, and #3 are identical, as are triangles #2 and #4.

1. To make triangle #1 cut 1¾″ wide strips of cloth in the following lengths:

Turquoise (T)	68¼″	O	45½″	Y	22¾″
Maroon (M)	66½″	Navy (N)	43¾″	Green (G)	21″
Pale Pink (PP)	64¾″	Pink (P)	42″	Y	19¼″
Red (R)	63″	N	40¼″	G	17½″
PP	61¼″	P	38½″	PP	15¾″
R	59½″	T	36¾″	N	14″
Yellow (Y)	57¾″	M	35″	PP	12¼″
T	56″	T	33¼″	N	10½″
Y	54¼″	M	31½″	O	8¾″
T	52½″	W	29¾″	W	7″
White (W)	50¾″	R	28″	O	5¼″
Orange (O)	49″	W	26¼″	W	3½″
W	47¼″	R	24½″	O	1¾″

step 2

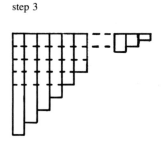

2. Sew the strips together in the order listed above. The assembled strips will look like the opposite diagram.

3. Cut across the strips to create new strips, each 1¾″ wide and consisting of a string of square elements.

step 3

4. Sew the new strips together, aligning their right edges and seams. This operation will create a one-step shift in the colored elements. The left edge will have a zig-zag shape and the colored squares will also zig-zag across the field. This is triangle #1.

5. To make triangle #2, cut 1¾″ wide strips of cloth in the following lengths:

step 4

Turquoise (T)	68¼″	R	59½″	White (W)	50¾″
Maroon (M)	66½″	Yellow (Y)	57¾″	Orange (O)	49″
Pale Pink (PP)	64¾″	T	56″	W	47¼″
Red (R)	63″	Y	54¼″	O	45½″
PP	61¼″	T	52½″	Navy (N)	43¾″

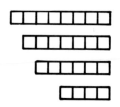

Pink (P)	42″		R	28″		N	14″	
N	40¼″		W	26¼″		PP	12¼″	
P	38½″		R	24½″		N	10½″	
T	36¾″		Y	22¾″		O	8¾″	
M	35″		Green (G)	21″		W	7″	
T	33¼″		Y	19¼″		O	5¼″	
M	31½″		G	17½″		T	3½″	
W	29¾″		PP	15¾″		P	1¾″	

step 10

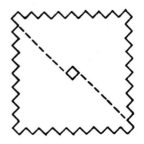

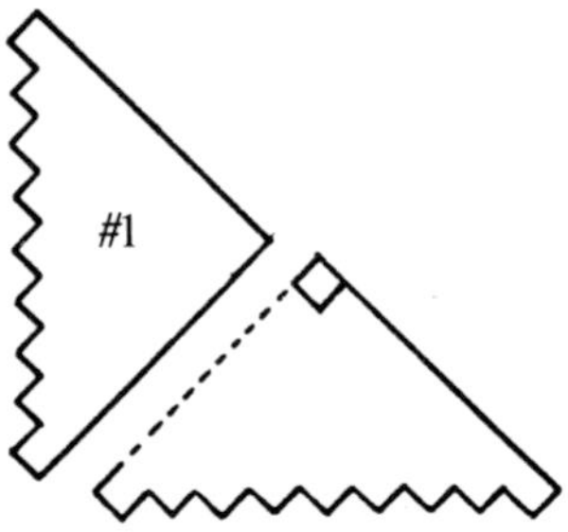

6. Follow instructions for assembly of triangle #1.

7. Create triangle #3. It is identical to triangle #1.

8. Create triangle #4. It is identical to triangle #2.

step 11

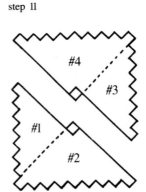

9. Pin triangle #1 to triangle #2, offsetting by one square. That is, position the first turquoise element of #2 under the first maroon element of #1. Note that the last pink square of #2 will have no mate. Sew.

10. Repeat step 9 with triangles #3 and #4.

11. Lay the two large pieces next to each other with their single pink sqaures overlapping each other.

12. Pin straight edges together as shown. Sew two seams, one seam joining triangle #1 to #4; the other joining #2 to #3.

step 12

13. There will be an unfinished hole at the middle of the quilt where the two pink elements overlap. Turn the seam allowance under on the top square, and sew it by hand over the bottom pink square.

14. Lay the piecework on a large white backing cloth. Fold the backing up and over to create the borders. Miter the edges and sew.

Tiare Tahiti

If one had to choose the most popular design of all, it would be the Tiare Tahiti pattern. This motif is so prevalent and so traditional that it is almost synonymous with the term *tifaifai*. The tiare Tahiti is a small form of gardenia, bearing an average of six to eight petals. A deceptively simple and unassuming flower, it has a powerfully sweet fragrance and figures heavily in Tahitian legends. Tiare Tahiti was once called *tiare Maohi*. Maohi is what the Tahitian calls himself and it is a word that embodies both the person and the Polynesian lifestyle. This flower was associated with the old gods and was so important that ten stages of the flower's development and decline were identified and given distinct names. Used as an ingredient in medicine, as a perfume for coconut oil, and as the preferred flower for heis, the tiare Tahiti is also the theme of countless island love songs.

In most cases, this motif represents the bud stage of the flower, considered the best stage for wearing, for fragrance, and for its reputed medicinal properties. The quilt pattern is well balanced and uses about 128 buds to form the central design and inner border. Some Tiare Tahiti patterns may use hundreds of tiny buds to form the design, while others are extremely simple. This motif is traditionally made with a green background and white appliquéd top which are in keeping with the natural colors of the flower. Blue and white, as shown here, and red and white are also seen from time to time. It is unusual to find the tiare bud made in colors other than white, although some innovations in color appear now and then. For the most part, they are considered less pleasing than the traditional green and white. *Made by Jean Mercier, Vahine Poerani Association.*

Dimensions: 8' × 7'

With the exception of the outermost scalloped border, this design is cut as one piece. There are three concentric rings of buds. Each ring is joined horizontally and vertically by a narrow band of cloth. The inner border is an extension of the largest circle and is joined by ten strips of cloth.

Fold the base fabric and top fabric in fourths and press them lightly. This will help to accurately center the pattern. Fold the cloth with the single folded edge kept to your left. Transfer the pattern with carbon paper. Use lots of pins to secure the layers together. Begin cutting the scalloped border. The rest of the pattern is cut from the outer edges toward the center of the quilt. Leave at least ¼ " allowance. There are many narrow spaces to cut, so keep the cutting line simple and go slowly.

Attach the scalloped border to the base fabric and match all creases. Place the cutout design on the base fabric and open in half. Carefully peel back the top of the design, matching horizontal and vertical creases. Thumbtack the creases down to the table. Pin and baste that half of the pattern. Then shift the material on the table, and pin and baste that half. Every slit should be basted. When doing appliqué stitches, keep small scissors handy to notch troublesome curves.

Graph pattern:
1 square = 1⅜"

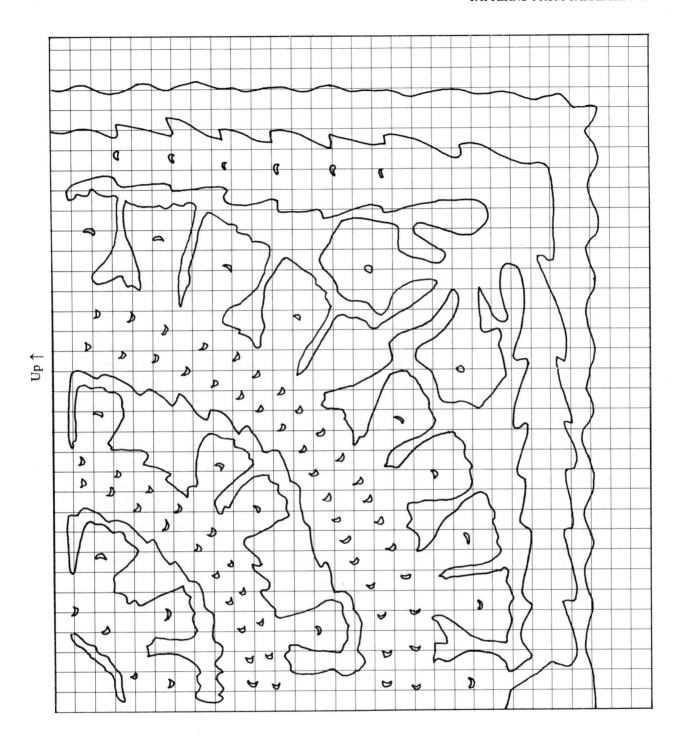

Orchide

Orchide is an exquisite example of the tifaifai mosaic style. It was designed by a woman transplanted to Tahiti from another island of French Polynesia. Because of inter-island travel and resettlement, the various needlework styles and techniques of eastern Polynesia have blended and overlapped. Piecework mosaics are made by the Tahitian people, but have not reached the level of specialty found in Rurutu and the nearby Tuamotu islands, with one exception, the island of Raiatea. In Rurutu, these mosaics are called by two names, tifaifai pu, as a general term, and *iripiti*, a more specialized name.

Although this design is credited to one woman and could have been made alone, there appears to be some diagonal movement in the patchwork which indicates that the stitching may have been done by more than one person. Polynesian patchwork is often made as a cooperative effort. This tifaifai is a small one, measuring approximately 6½′ × 7′, but the complexity of the pattern and the many small patches used suggest that anyone re-creating the design should seek assistance.

Voluptuous use of color creates soft shadows and vibrant highlights in this bouquet of orchids. The floral motif set within black patchwork creates depth and a three-dimensional quality. On first examination, it seems as though the flowers have been appliquéd to a solid back because black piecework recedes. The ability to visualize the pattern, coordinate the patches, and set them down in such painterly fashion is greatly admired by Tahitian artisans and such a tifaifai is highly valued. *Made by Colette Tehahe, Areratai Tamarii Association, Rurutu.*

Dimensions: approximately 7' × 6½'

The quilt has 6″ borders on the left and right and 3″ borders on the top and bottom. Some of the pieced rows are obscured by the borders which have been folded over and stitched down. Orchide is made of 8,400 square elements in eight different colors. Certain colors have two or three shades, but these subtle variations are not reproduced in the following instructions.

1. The basic element is a square block which measures 1⅜″ × 1⅜″. After the ¼″ seams are sewn, the element size on the quilt top will be ⅞″ × ⅞″.

2. Cut 1⅜″-square elements of the following colors:

Green (G)	Navy or	Yellow (Y)
Lime Green (L)	royal blue (N)	Maroon (M)
Black (B)	Orange (O)	Pink (P)

3. The quilt is assembled by sewing squares together to make long strips. Each strip is 84 squares long.

4. The first strip is at the left edge, running vertically from lower to upper corner. The sequence of elements is: 37 Black (B), 2 lime green (L), and 45 black (B).

5. Sew the remaining strips:

Strip

   2. 36B, 3L, 1M, 2L, 42B

   3. 35B, 4L, 1M, 3L, 10B, 4P, 27B

   4. 34B, 5L, 2M, 3L, 7B, 5N, 3P, 25B

   5. 33B, 6L, 2M, 4L, 5B, 1M, 7N, 4P, 22B

   6. 1L, 31B, 1M, 6L, 2M, 4L, 4B, 9M, 1N, 4P, 21B

   7. 2L, 30B, 1M, 6L, 2M, 5L, 3B, 10M, 4P, 21B

   8. 3L, 28B, 1M, 7L, 3M, 5L, 2B, 10M, 2N, 2P, 21B

   9. 2L, 1G, 28B, 1M, 7L, 3M, 6L, 1B, 10M, 2B, 2P, 21B

  10. 2L, 2G, 27B, 1M, 7L, 3M, 1L, 5M, 2B, 2N, 7M, 2B, 3P, 20B

  11. 2L, 4G, 24B, 1M, 8L, 9M, 5N, 6M, 2N, 4P, 19B

12. 7G, 3B, 4M, 16B, 2M, 7L, 9M, 1N, 2P, 2N, 6M, 2N, 3M, 2P, 18B

13. 8G, 3B, 10M, 9B, 2M, 7L, 7M, 1P, 4M, 1P, 2N, 11M, 3P, 16B

14. 8G, 5B, 8M, 9B, 3M, 4L, 8M, 1P, 2N, 1P, 1N, 2M, 2N, 11M, 1N, 2P, 16B

15. 9G, 4B, 12M, 6B, 2M, 4L, 4M, 2P, 1M, 1P, 5N, 2M, 1P, 1N, 11M, 2N, 2P, 15B

16. 9G, 2B, 3M, 7L, 7M, 3B, 2M, 3L, 3M, 2P, 2N, 1P, 6N, 2M, 1P, 2M, 1P, 1N, 8M, 2N, 3P, 14B

17. 9G, 1B, 2M, 17L, 3B, 2M, 2L, 3M, 2P, 2N, 1P, 1N, 7M, 1P, 1M, 3P, 1N, 7M, 2N, 4P, 6B, 7L

18. 1L, 7G, 8M, 14L, 3B, 1M, 1L, 3M, 2P, 6N, 6M, 1P, 1N, 4P, 1N, 6M, 2N, 5P, 3B, 9L

19. 2L, 7G, 4L, 9M, 9L, 2B, 1M, 1L, 3M, 2P, 5N, 8M, 5P, 1N, 6M, 3N, 5P, 1B, 7L, 3G

20. 17G, 7M, 7G, 2B, 2M, 1P, 6N, 11M, 3P, 1N, 2P, 1N, 3M, 4N, 5P, 2B, 5L, 5G

21. 20G, 7M, 5G, 2B, 1P, 1N, 4M, 2N, 1M, 3P, 7M, 2P, 2N, 2P, 1N, 3M, 5N, 5P, 1B, 5L, 5G

22. 23G, 6M, 3G, 3P, 1N, 9M, 1P, 7M, 2P, 1N, 3P, 1N, 3M, 7N, 3P, 5L, 6G

23. 4G, 5L, 15G, 16M, 2G, 1P, 1M, 1P, 1N, 1M, 2P, 14M, 3N, 4P, 1N, 2M, 6N, 3P, 5L, 7G

24. 1L, 2G, 1L, 5N, 1L, 14G, 7M, 1G, 1P, 2M, 1N, 1M, 2P, 9M, 12P, 1N, 2M, 5N, 6P, 5L, 8G

25. 1N, 1L, 1G, 7N, 1L, 14G, 7M, 1P, 4M, 3P, 7M, 13P, 1N, 2M, 4N, 4P, 4L, 9G

26. 2N, 1L, 10N, 6M, 5G, 8M, 1P, 4M, 4P, 6M, 2P, 2N, 10P, 1N, 1M, 4N, 3P, 4L, 9G, 1B

27. 14N, 18M, 3P, 2M, 5P, 4M, 2P, 1N, 2P, 3N, 7P, 1N, 1M, 3N, 3P, 5L, 9G, 1B

28. 16N, 5M, 8N, 3M, 1G, 3P, 1M, 6P, 3M, 2P, 1N, 5P, 1N, 6P, 1N, 3M, 1N, 3P, 2L, 12G, 1B

29. 17N, 3M, 10N, 1M, 2G, 4P, 1N, 5P, 3M, 2P, 1N, 5P, 1N, 6P, 1N, 2M, 18G, 2B

30. 18N, 1G, 12N, 3G, 3P, 1N, 5P, 2M, 3P, 1N, 12P, 1N, 1M, 1N, 6P, 9G, 5B

31. 18N, 1G, 12N, 3G, 3P, 2N, 5P, 1M, 3P, 1N, 10P, 2N, 2M, 1N, 6P, 14B

32. 18N, 1G, 12N, 4G, 3P, 1N, 5P, 1N, 3P, 1N, 8P, 4N, 2M, 5N, 2P, 14B

33. 3N, 4O, 24N, 4G, 3P, 2N, 4P, 1N, 3P, 2N, 6P, 3N, 3M, 5N, 3P, 5G, 9B

34. 2N, 6O, 22N, 6G, 3P, 1N, 4P, 1N, 4P, 1N, 5P, 4N, 3M, 3N, 6P, 6G, 7B

35. 2N, 6O, 21N, 7G, 3P, 1N, 4P, 1N, 4P, 1N, 5P, 3N, 3M, 3N, 7P, 3G, 1L, 3G, 6B

36. 3N, 4O, 24N, 6G, 2P, 1N, 13P, 5N, 2M, 2N, 8P, 3G, 4L, 3G, 4B

37. 3N, 4O, 15N, 2O, 8N, 5G, 14P, 6N, 3M, 2N, 7P, 4G, 6L, 2G, 3B

38. 4N, 3O, 14N, 5O, 7N, 4G, 1P, 1M, 12P, 4N, 6M, 2N, 5P, 14G, 2B

39. 21N, 6O, 7N, 3G, 3M, 10P, 4N, 7M, 2N, 5P, 3L, 6G, 3L, 3G, 1B

40. 21N, 6O, 7N, 3G, 6M, 5P, 5N, 4M, 1N, 3M, 2N, 5P, 5L, 4G, 4L, 2G, 1B

41. 2G, 3N, 9O, 6N, 5O, 8N, 3G, 10M, 5N, 5M, 4N, 6P, 6L, 3G, 4L, 2G

42. 2G, 2N, 10O, 3G, 4N, 3Y, 9N, 3G, 1P, 15M, 2N, 1M, 2N, 1P, 3N, 2M, 6P, 7L, 4G, 2L, 2G

43. 2G, 1N, 3O, 4N, 4O, 2G, 17N, 4G, 1P, 3N, 4M, 1P, 4M, 4N, 1M, 1N, 3P, 2N, 2M, 5P, 10L, 6G

44. 2G, 1N, 2O, 6N, 3O, 1G, 17N, 6G, 1P, 6N, 1P, 3M, 6N, 4P, 4N, 5P, 12L, 4G

45. 2G, 1N, 1O, 8N, 1O, 1G, 10N, 1G, 7N, 3G, 3Y, 2P, 1Y, 1P, 3N, 1G, 1M, 8N, 7P, 1N, 5P, 13L, 3G

46. 2G, 1O, 21N, 2G, 5N, 3G, 10N, 6Y, 3P, 3G, 7N, 13P, 14L, 3G

47. 3G, 21N, 3G, 3N, 3G, 3O, 9Y, 1O, 2G, 18P, 16L, 2G

48. 3G, 21N, 9G, 3O, 9Y, 2O, 2G, 8P, 5Y, 2O, 3G, 16L, 1G

49. 1G, 2B, 7N, 1O, 13N, 9G, 3O, 10Y, 2O, 2G, 6P, 6Y, 4O, 2G, 15L, 1G

50. 4B, 6N, 1O, 12N, 10G, 3O, 11Y, 1O, 3G, 5P, 6Y, 1O, 2Y, 2O, 2G, 15L

51. 6B, 3N, 3O, 10N, 9G, 2Y, 3O, 12Y, 1O, 3G, 3P, 8Y, 1O, 1Y, 2O, 4G, 13L

52. 3B, 6N, 4O, 8N, 8G, 5Y, 2O, 12Y, 1O, 4G, 2O, 8Y, 1O, 2Y, 2O, 5G, 11L

53. 1B, 8N, 4Y, 2O, 6N, 7G, 6Y, 2O, 11Y, 2O, 3G, 2O, 9Y, 1O, 3Y, 1O, 8G, 8B

54. 8N, 1O, 5Y, 1O, 7N, 10G, 7Y, 2O, 9Y, 3O, 2G, 3O, 9Y, 2O, 2Y, 2O, 6G, 9B

55. 5N, 4O, 5Y, 1O, 8N, 4G, 9Y, 2O, 8Y, 4O, 1G, 2O, 10Y, 2O, 3Y, 1O, 5G, 10B

56. 8N, 2O, 4Y, 1O, 9N, 3G, 8Y, 3O, 8Y, 6O, 11Y, 2O, 3Y, 2O, 3G, 11B

57. 10N, 3Y, 2O, 9N, 4G, 6Y, 5O, 7Y, 3O, 1Y, 1M, 12Y, 3O, 3Y, 1O, 2G, 12B

58. 10N, 5O, 9N, 5G, 4Y, 8O, 5Y, 3O, 1Y, 6M, 8Y, 3O, 2Y, 2O, 1G, 12B

59. 13N, 3O, 8N, 6G, 3Y, 2O, 4M, 10O, 1Y, 7M, 9Y, 3O, 1Y, 1O, 1G, 12B

60. 1B, 14N, 2O, 6N, 8G, 2Y, 2O, 5M, 9O, 1Y, 5M, 3O, 9Y, 4O, 1G, 2L, 10B

61. 2B, 14N, 1O, 5N, 10G, 1Y, 3O, 5M, 8O, 1Y, 4M, 17O, 1G, 5L, 7B

62. 3B, 2L, 3G, 9N, 2G, 2B, 13G, 6O, 1M, 1O, 13M, 16O, 5L, 3G, 5B

63. 2B, 2L, 4G, 9N, 2G, 2B, 14G, 7O, 14M, 15O, 7L, 6G

64. 1B, 2L, 5G, 9N, 2G, 1B, 7G, 6O, 2Y, 1G, 4O, 2M, 9O, 2M, 2O, 3M, 12O, 10L, 1G, 1L, 2G

65. 1B, 2L, 6G, 8N, 2G, 1B, 5G, 10O, 2Y, 2O, 1M, 16O, 4M, 9O, 13L, 2G

66. 2L, 7G, 6N, 4G, 1B, 4G, 34O, 3M, 8O, 12L, 3B

67. 2L, 8G, 4N, 5G, 1B, 4G, 19O, 3Y, 1O, 1Y, 10O, 4M, 1O, 2M, 1L, 1O, 13L, 4B

68. 1L, 1B, 16G, 2B, 3G, 4O, 1Y, 14O, 7Y, 11O, 5M, 14L, 5B

69. 1L, 1B, 6G, 1L, 9G, 4B, 1G, 4O, 2Y, 2O, 1Y, 2O, 1M, 5O, 12Y, 9O, 17L, 6B

70. 2B, 5G, 2L, 8G, 3B, 2G, 7Y, 1O, 2Y, 1O, 1M, 5O, 13Y, 9O, 16L, 7B

71. 8L, 8G, 3B, 3G, 9Y, 1O, 1M, 4O, 16Y, 8O, 1Y, 13L, 8B

72. 8L, 7G, 3B, 5G, 8Y, 2O, 1M, 3O, 18Y, 8O, 10L, 11B

73. 7L, 6G, 4B, 7G, 6Y, 2O, 1M, 3O, 19Y, 8O, 1Y, 7L, 13G

74. 6B, 4G, 7B, 7G, 6Y, 2O, 1M, 2O, 21Y, 8O, 1Y 17L, 2G

75. 16B, 8G, 5Y, 3O, 1M, 21Y, 2M, 9O, 4L, 6B, 7L, 2G

76. 16B, 8G, 4Y, 4O, 1M, 10Y, 2M, 8Y, 5M, 7O, 5L, 14B

77. 15B, 8G, 4Y, 5O, 1M, 10Y, 3M, 5Y, 8M, 2O, 3Y, 8L, 12B

78. 13B, 10G, 7Y, 3O, 1G, 9Y, 3M, 2Y, 1M, 1Y, 6M, 1O, 4M, 2Y, 6L, 1B, 4L, 10B

79. 18B, 5G, 8Y, 2O, 1G, 5Y, 7M, 1Y, 6M, 6O, 4Y, 7L, 2B, 3L, 9B

80. 9B, 8G, 6L, 2G, 7Y, 3O, 2Y, 15M, 7O, 4Y, 1G, 6L, 3B, 2L, 9B

81. 7B, 13G, 4L, 2G, 8Y, 2G, 4M, 6O, 5M, 8O, 3Y, 1G, 3B, 4L, 4B, 2L, 8B

82. 6B, 3G, 13L, 4G, 2B, 1G, 3B, 4G, 23O, 2Y, 2G, 11B, 4L, 6B

83. 4B, 3G, 8L, 9G, 2B, 9G, 2Y, 2O, 1Y, 11O, 1Y, 7O, 2Y, 1L, 13B, 4G, 5B

84. 4B, 3G, 3L, 13G, 2B, 10G, 2Y, 3O, 1Y, 11O, 1Y, 6O, 1Y, 2L, 14B, 4G, 4B

85. 3B, 3G, 9L, 7G, 2B, 11G, 3Y, 3O, 1Y, 17O, 1Y, 2L, 14B, 4G, 4B

86. 3B, 1G, 9L, 5G, 2L, 3B, 4G, 1L, 2G, 2L, 4G, 3Y, 8O, 3Y, 9O, 1Y, 1L, 16B, 2G, 5B

87. 2B, 2G, 7L, 4G, 4L, 2B, 3G, 4L, 2G, 2L, 1G, 1B, 3G, 3Y, 7O, 4Y, 7O, 2Y, 1L, 16B, 1G, 6B

88. 2B, 1G, 6L, 4G, 6L, 4G, 5L, 2G, 2L, 1G, 5B, 4Y, 3O, 8Y, 4O, 2Y 2L 23B

89. 1B, 2G, 5L, 2G, 7L, 6G, 4L, 2G, 4L, 1G, 5B, 9Y, 3L, 7Y, 2L, 24B

90. 1B, 1G, 5L, 3G, 9L, 4G, 4L, 2G, 4L, 1G, 6B, 7Y, 5L, 5Y, 3L, 24B

91. 2G, 4L, 3G, 9L, 2B, 3G, 4L, 2G, 4L, 2G, 6B, 3Y, 8L, 4Y, 3L 25B

92. 2G, 3L, 3G, 10L, 3B, 2G, 5L, 1G, 5L, 1G, 5L, 1G, 7B, 4L, 2B, 11L, 25B

93. 1G, 4L, 1G, 11L, 4B, 2G, 5L, 1G, 5L, 8B, 3L, 3B, 10L, 26B

94. 1G, 15L, 5B, 2G, 4L, 2G, 5L, 9B, 1L, 4B, 10L, 26B

95. 15L, 6B, 2G, 4L, 1G, 6L, 14B, 9L, 27B

96. 4L, 3B, 3L, 11B, 2G, 3L, 2G, 5L, 16B, 8L, 27B

97. 2L, 20B, 1G, 3L, 1G, 5L, 17B, 7L, 28B

98. 22B, 2G, 8L, 18B, 5L, 29B

99. 23B, 2G, 6L, 19B, 5L, 29B

100. 24B, 2G, 5L, 20B, 3L, 30B

7. Sew the strips together in the proper order, carefully matching seams.

8. Complete the quilt by adding borders and backing.

Roti (B)

This brilliant red on pink design is the most traditional handling of the Roti (rose) motif. The late introduction of roses to Tahiti, combined with increasingly conventionalized appliqué techniques popular in the mid-1800s, resulted in the rose motif being found almost exclusively in appliquéd tifaifai, rather than piecework. The appliquéd rose motif is done in a variety of ways and is often far more ornate than the quilt shown here. Although this design is simple, it is a pure and strong example of Tahitian appliqué, made in the tifaifai pa'oti style, as opposed to the first Roti project (pp. 64-67), which is made in the Rarotongan style. By Polynesian standards, this second pattern follows the rules of good design. It is bold, the colors are bright and highly contrasting, there is little empty space within the design, and there is a sense of flatness or two-dimensionality.

The exuberant pink and red are representative of the colors of the rose and are also an expression of the Tahitian love of bright colors. There is a pleasing thorny look to the design. To achieve it, jagged edges of the thorns should be cut out as bluntly as possible to allow room for turning the fabric into sharp points. The simplicity of this tifaifai makes it a good project for the person with beginning appliqué skills. *Made by Therese Atani, Hapaiano Association, Papenoo.*

Dimensions: 8' × 7'

Rose motifs will keep a characteristic Tahitian flavor if made in bright colors. Common colors are pink on green, red on yellow, and maroon on beige.

Place the 8' measurement horizontally and fold in half toward you. Fold in half again, keeping the single folded edge to the left. The scalloped border is drawn along the loose edges of the cloth. When cut it will open into one piece. Secure the rose design with pins and cut from the outer edges toward the center. Leave at least ¼" allowance, more when cutting out the sharp points. The slits in the roses should be cut as a straight line.

Open the base fabric wrong side up. Lay the border on the base fabric, also wrong side up. Match all creases, pin, and sew all straight edges. Fold the border over to the right side, pin, and baste the scalloped edges down.

Place the rose pattern on the fabric. Open in half and match all central creases. Tack the creases down. Pin and baste the design from the center and work out, keeping the material flat.

Graph pattern:
1 square = 1⅜"

Up ↑

Tahirihiri

This Tahirihiri pattern of fans is an echo of the old appliqué patterns believed to have originated with the arii, the royal chiefs. On some of the Society Islands, fans were symbols of the nobility. The colors are the traditional Tahitian quilting colors—red and white. Before the advent of Europeans, red was an important decorative color used for the tapa worn by chiefs and in the red feathered *maro*, the girdle, which signified both secular and supernatural power. Much of the early trade cloth brought by merchant ships was a red cloth called "Turkey Red." Red and white cloth was so predominant that most designs in the early 1800s were executed in those colors.

Tahirihiri means fans, but in modern usage, often refers to the style of the tifaifai rather than the actual pattern. Tahirihiri designs are always intricate with many edges to be sewn down. When questioned, the artisans were unanimous in their declarations that these patterns are the most difficult to make. One woman told a story about how four women spent two days basting down a particularly intricate motif.

All parts of the design are joined together in this pattern. The small red inner border is cut out as part of the central design, unlike many tifaifai whose borders are cut separately and attached as a separate design element. The white framing border, which is the background fabric, is a simple version of the straight-edged white border found on many old tifaifai. The tahirihiri style requires very careful drawing, cutting, and basting. When basting the cutout design to the backing, care must be taken that every cut edge is secured. This tifaifai should be attempted by quilters already skilled in appliqué technique. *Made by Sophie Aro, Tamarii Atehi Association, Punaaia.*

Dimensions: 8' × 7'

The white fabric measures 8' × 7'. The finished size of the red fabric is 6½' × 5½'. Buy a couple of extra inches of the red fabric. The final size of the enlarged pattern graph should be about 3¼' × 2¾'. The smaller size of the pattern and the complexity of the design makes this project suitable for the experienced hand. Use high quality cotton to prevent fraying during appliqué.

Place the 6½' measurement of the red cloth vertically. Fold this in half, toward you. Fold in half again, with the single fold kept to the left. Transfer the pattern with carbon and pin the design down well. Cut the outer edges of the scalloping first. Leave ¼" allowance. Then cut the inner edges of the scalloping. Be careful not to separate the design from the border. Tahirihiri style requires that small bits of cloth are cut and lifted out of the design.

After cutting, open the base fabric and place the half-open design on top. Center all creases. Peel back the top layer and tack the creases to the table every few inches. Pin and baste that half of the design. Every slit must be basted. Work from the center out. Complete the rest of the design in the same manner.

Graph pattern:
1 square = 1⅜"

Up ↑

Te Mori

The lamp, Te Mori, has been an important part of Tahitian life and culture since its introduction. According to tradition, only a lamp stood between the well-being of the Tahitian family and the *tupapa'u*, the restless spirits of ancestors believed to roam the night. The artist Paul Gauguin noted in his journal (written between 1891 and 1903) that no Tahitian would sleep without his lamp burning through the night. This customary precaution still is taken in some of the quiet neighboring islands and areas of eastern Polynesia. Before the lamp was introduced, islanders burned the hard nuts of the candlenut tree, which, when strung together and ignited, glow for several hours.

The lamp is set off by fern leaves, called *maire*, which provide a decorative and festive touch. The inner sawtooth border of brown is cut as part of the central design, while the orange border is the base fabric. The brown border that frames the whole quilt is cut from the folded fabric as a separate piece. This quilt has a strong regional flavor, both in motif and in the use of traditional earth tones. Its pattern is an example of the tahirihiri style tifaifai. Careful appliqué technique and a sure hand are needed to make the quilt, particularly in the lamp portion of the design. *Made by Millia Ebbs, Teva I Tai Association, Vairao.*

Dimensions: 8' × 7'

This is another pattern that is best tried on paper before cutting it in cloth. Lay the fabric open with the 8' length placed horizontally and fold in half, bringing it toward you. Fold again and keep the single fold to the left. Once the design is transferred to the cloth with carbon, pin all layers well. Begin cutting the dog-tooth border on the outside first. Then trim the sawtooth edges of the inner border.

In cutting the pattern, keep the cutting line very simple. Start with the outline of the lamp, leaving a ¼ " allowance all around. Snip out the small openings and the interior of the lamp. Fold the lamp back and out of the way. The serrated leaves are cut as diagonal lines and will be turned into shape later.

Open the base fabric wrong side up and attach the border, also wrong side up. Match all creases and stitch the straight edges. Turn the border over to the right side and baste. Place the cutout design on the base fabric and center the creases. Gradually peel back the top part of the design and tack down the creases. Pin and baste all edges. The rest of the design is shifted on the table and finished in the same way.

Graph pattern:
1 square = 1⅜″

Up ↑

Anthuriums

The flamboyant anthurium flower, long associated with the Hawaiian islands, is a recent introduction to Tahiti. It now thrives in the Tahitian soil and climate and is grown by local flower vendors. Although Tahiti has a wealth of native flowers, islanders frequently buy bouquets of anthuriums to brighten their homes and offices. The anthurium is a waxy, heart-shaped flower with a thick protruding stamen. Though it has no fragrance, it is popular for its bright red color. Mellower shades of yellow, pink, and white are grown in Tahiti as well.

Two devices are used in this Anthurium pattern: folded cutouts and templates. The border flows around the tifaifai, erupting into clusters of leaves in the four corners. It is cut from the edges of the folded fabric. The central leaf design is also cut from folded cloth and, in this pattern, is not joined to the rest of the design. The anthurium templates are placed in a perfect balance of size and color, and the deep blue background fabric, overlaid with dark green, gives the flowers a vivid and almost three-dimensional quality. This tifaifai is an example of modern trends that are showing up in Tahitian quilting. Using multicolored flowers as part of the overall design is not traditional, yet the resulting quilt has the look of a more conventional tifaifai. *Made by Nadia Parau, Tiare Taina Uumu Association, Toahotu.*

Dimensions: 8' × 7'

In this pattern the leaves and border are cut from folded cloth. The flowers are made with templates, but most Tahitian artisans draw the flower shapes on folded cloth and cut them out four at a time.

There are twelve yellow flowers (eight large, four small); sixteen yellow stamens (twelve large and four small); sixteen pink flowers (twelve large and four small); and four large pink stamens. The pink stamens are appliquéd in an intermediate size. There are sixteen red flowers (four large and twelve medium); twenty-four red stamens (sixteen large and eight small); twelve white flowers (eight large and four medium); and twelve white stamens (eight large and four small). The large flowers are 6″ from tip to tip. The medium flowers measure 4½″, the small flowers, 3″. The stamens measure 3½″ and 2½″.

For the border and leaves, fold the fabric in fourths. The 8′ measurement is horizontal. Fold toward you. Fold in half again and keep the single fold to the left. Cut the border out first. Then cut the central leaf design. Open the base fabric wrong side up and center the border, also wrong side up. Stitch, turn it up and over, and baste down. Center the leaf design with the creases and baste down. Cut the flowers and stamens and arrange as shown. Baste all edges. Begin appliquéing from the center of the quilt.

Patterns are actual size.

Patterns are actual size.

Graph pattern pieces:
1 square = $1\frac{3}{8}''$

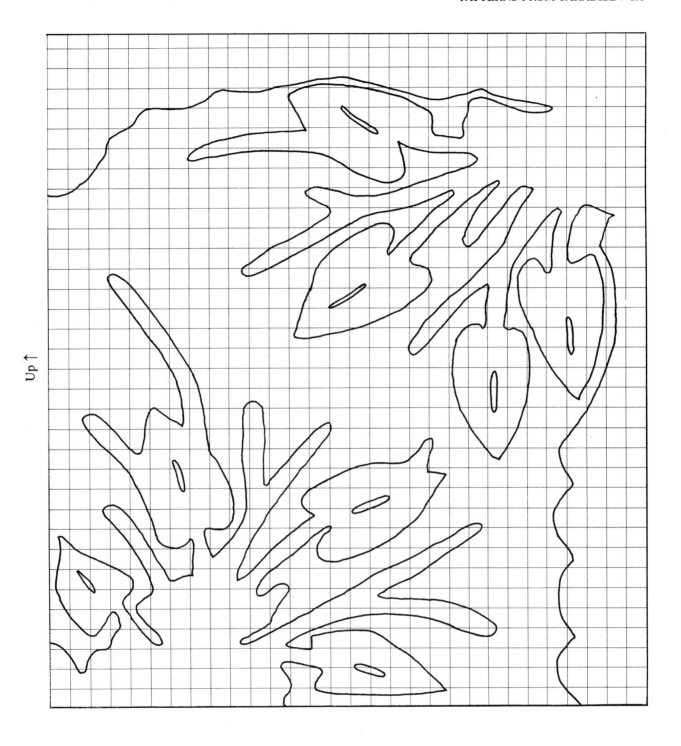

Up ↑

Hei Tiare

This elegant design is another old pattern made in traditional red and white. Hei Tiare is sometimes made in green and white to accurately represent the green fern leaves, called maire, and the buds of the white tiare Tahiti flower. The hei is a decoration worn as a wreath around the head. The pattern is sometimes called Tiare No Maire, tiare with fern.

Heis are made with any possible combination of flowers, ferns, leaves, or shells and are universally worn by Tahitian men, women, and children. They are prominently displayed during festivities and are also worn as everyday adornment. Flowers are collected from the garden and quickly woven into heis freshly made each morning. The hei tiare is considered the king of heis and was traditionally worn by the Tahitian arii. It shades the eyes from the sun, looks wonderful, and smells divine.

The two sides of the hei curve around a central medallion. The medallion is thought to be a remnant of early quilting designs taught by missionaries. The fern leaves should be cut out square, leaving ample room to turn under the points while sewing. Careful basting of this design is essential. While appliquéing, turn back the edges with the side of the needle, taking care to keep the outlines of the flower buds very thin and controlled for the proper effect. *Made by Mahine Ti-paon, Te Fare Vahine A Tahu Association, Tautira.*

Dimensions: 8' × 7'

To make this pattern sucessfully, proceed slowly and carefully during each stage. Two pairs of scissors may be helpful—fabric shears and small needlework or buttonhole scissors. It might be wise to practice the transfer and cutting of this design on paper before cutting the cloth.

Once the design is transferred to the cloth, pin the layers together, using lots of pins to control the fabric during the cutting stage.

Cut the border off first and then work toward the center. There are ten buds within the fern leaves and one at the corner of the folded edges. Pinch the material up and take a snip. Cut the outline of the buds as a simple, blunt W shape. The slits within the buds are pinched up and snipped as a short straight line.

Affix the border wrong side up to the base fabric, also wrong side up. Sew the perimeters, turn up and over, and baste down. Then place the center medallion in the exact center of the quilt, secure it, and baste. The other pattern pieces should be arranged as shown in the color photograph, using generous basting.

Graph pattern:
1 square = $1\frac{3}{8}''$

Up ↑

Pūpū

Cone shells, cowries, augers, and helmets—the shells of Tahiti are rich and varied. As befitting an island culture, shells have been an important element in decorative arts from ancient times. Taking advantage of nature's abundance, the Tahitians have transformed shells into jewelry, heis, percussion instruments, and even a means of communication by blowing into large shells as horns. The shell motif in this tifaifai, Pūpū, is a representation of Triton's Trumpet, a large shell valuable to collectors.

The arrangement of shells is reminiscent of a view through a kaleidoscope. There is a carefully planned symmetry visible in the outermost grouping of shells which is both part of the design and a framing border. The twists and curves of the individual shells have been formed by making small slits in the yellow cloth which is turned back to reveal the red fabric. These two colors are traditional, going back to pre-European days. The use of these colors gives the design more importance and the tifaifai, as a whole, a feeling of formality.

Although the technique used is traditional—the pattern is cut out from folded cloth—it is unusual to have shells depicted this way. They are more often seen as scattered design elements. Exactness in cutting, centering, and basting will prevent an off-center look. One of the arrow shapes radiating from the center of the design has been misplaced, an indication that the designer and the stitcher were not the same person. *Made by André Lehartel, Tiare Rau Artisanal Association, Papara.*

Dimensions: 8′ × 7′

This tifaifai can be difficult to cut: it may be best to try it on paper first. Place the open fabric with the 8′ dimensions set vertically and fold it down toward you. Fold it in half again, keeping the single folded edge to the left.

Enlarge the graph and transfer the pattern using carbon paper. Cut the border along the loose edges of the folded cloth. Lots of pins are needed to keep the shells together in the four layers of fabric. Cut slowly and carefully in the narrow spaces where the shells are joined together and near the folded edges. There are about twenty-five small openings in each shell. These are pinched up between the fingers and cut as short, curving slits.

Place the base fabric and border wrong side up and stitch the edges. Turn the border up and over and baste down. Place the cutout design on the base fabric and open in half. Center the pattern. Peel back the top of the cloth and thumbtack the creases in turn. Pin and baste all edges, working out from the center. Complete the rest of the design the same way.

Graph pattern:
1 square = 1⅜″

Up ↑

Te Moemoea No Iotefa

Even though tifaifai sprang from missionary origins, surprisingly few patterns reflect their religious beginnings. This tifaifai is one of the few and is known as Joseph's Dream or Te Moemoea No Iotefa. The pattern is an interpretation of the Biblical story of Joseph, found in Genesis, Chapter 37. Joseph's dreams and his ability to interpret them are translated into an appealing design. Depicted are moons, stars, and sheaves of wheat, elements of two prophetic dreams that were fulfilled in Egypt during a great famine. Joseph's Dream is unique among appliquéd tifaifai. Customarily, appliqué designs are inspired by things in nature—the solid object, rather than the idea, concept, or legend. No one remembers who originated this design or just how old it is. Whoever designed it broke all the rules when setting the story down in cloth.

The pattern is made in the reverse appliqué style, using negative space to bring out the design. The blue cloth on top is cut to allow the white base fabric to show through. Sandwiched between the center design and the blue outside border is the white base fabric, which shows through as a sharply contrasting inner border and gives the design added vitality. Joseph's Dream is usually made in blue and gold or maroon and gold. Several women worked on this tifaifai, cooperating in cutting and basting. Careful pinning and basting is essential. *Made by Mahine Ti-paon, Myrna Ti-paon, Moeata Tia; Te Fare Vahine A Taho Association, Tautira.*

Dimensions: 8' × 7'

This is a reverse appliqué design. The top cloth is cut to allow the bottom cloth to show through. It would be best to transfer the pattern to paper first to test the cutting requirements. Use two pairs of scissors, one large, one small.

The cloth must match in size. Open the top fabric with the 8' length placed horizontally. Fold the 8' length in half, toward you. Fold in half again, keeping the single fold to the left. Transfer the pattern and pin the design down well. Snip the slits in the outer border first and cut that border off, leaving a ¼" allowance. Cut the scalloped edges of the main design. Work in toward the center of the quilt. Snip the tiny circles with the points of the small scissors in an X shape. The star shape is cut out and lifted from the design, leaving an allowance. The sheaves of wheat are cut as simple lines. The smallest circles, the grain, should be snipped with small scissors, making sure all layers are penetrated.

Attach the outer border to the base fabric. Center the top cloth, open in half, and peel back the top of the cloth. Thumbtack all creases to the table. Pin well, baste from the center, and work out. To appliqué, turn the edges back and stitch with a blind hem or small overcast stitch. Begin appliqué from the center.

Graph pattern:
1 square = 1⅜"

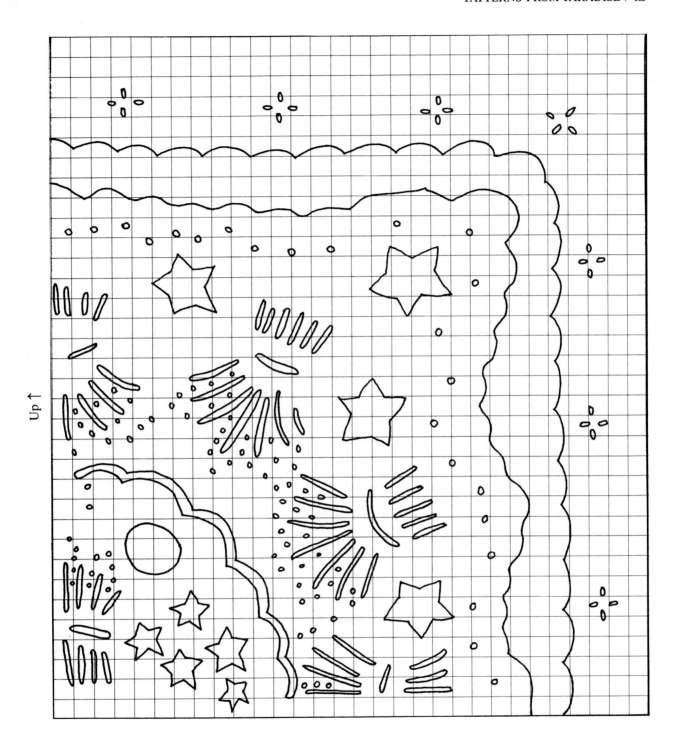

Up↑

Pronunciation Guide

The names of the patterns and other Tahitian words in the text will be easy to pronounce if a few simple rules are followed. There are eight consonants in the Tahitian language: *f, h, m, n, p, r, t,* and *v.* The vowels are *a, e, i, o,* and *u.* An apostrophe between letters indicates a pause or a glottal stop.

A is pronounced as *ah. E* is pronounced as *eh. I* is pronounced as *ee. O* is a short sound pronounced like the *o* in the word *off. U* is pronounced as *oo.* The *t* and *r* sounds are softer than in English. Adjacent vowels are pronounced with some blending of the two.

Glossary

Ahu. Tapa; bark cloth.

Ahufara. A large, square woman's shawl.

Arii. The royal wives of high chiefs; the highest class of chiefs, male or female.

Fare tamaara'a. Reception hall or feast house.

Fe'i. A type of banana.

Fetia. Star.

Hei. A head decoration made of flowers and worn as a wreath around the brow.

Heiva i Tahiti. Tahiti's festival.

Iripiti. Mosaic-patterned quilts, hand-pieced with very small squares.

Kapa. Hawaiian quilt.

Maire. Fern leaves.

Mama. An affectionate term for a Tahitian woman of middle age.

Mama ruau. Craftswomen.

Maro. Girdle.

Mauruuru. Thank you.

Meherio. Mermaid.

Mei'a. A type of banana.

Opuhi. A type of ginger; also refers to a pattern.

Pa'a honu. Sea turtle; also the name given to hexagon patchwork.

Pa'aro. A patchwork pattern similar to Drunkard's Path or Robbing Peter to Pay Paul.

Painapo. Pineapple.

Pandanus. A plant indigenous to most South Pacific islands.

Pa'oti. Cutting or scissors.

Pareu. A bold cotton-print cloth, worn as a body wrap by women.

Patu. Gathering; patchwork pattern resembling Log Cabin or Barn Raising.

Pu. Patchwork.

Pua. A trumpet-shaped flower native to the Society Islands; also a pattern derived from it.

Pua mahana. A type of sunflower.

Rimarima. Touching hands; a patchwork motif like Bear's Paw.

Roti. Rose.

Tahirihiri. Fan; also refers to a style of tifaifai intricately drawn and cut.

Tapa. Bark cloth.

Tapo'i. Special white tapa considered sacred.

Taratara. Star or half-star pillow.

Te miti. The sea.

Te Moemoea no Iotefa. Joseph's Dream.

Te Mori. The Lamp.

Te Vahine e te Miti. The Woman and the Sea.

Tiare. Flower; also refers to patterns derived from floral themes.

Tiare aute. Hibiscus.

Tiare no Maire. Tiare with Fern.

Tiare Tahiti. Gardenia.

Tifaifai. Appliquéd Tahitian quilt.

Tifaifai pu. Pieced Tahitian quilt.

Ti'i. Small religious statues.

Tipani. Frangipani.

Tiputa. A man's garment, similar to a poncho.

Tivaevae. Appliqué-style tifaifai made in the Cook Islands.

Tupapa'u. Restless spirits.

Uru. Breadfruit.

Vahine. Tahitian woman.

Vehituru'a. Pillowcase.

Bibliography

Barrau, J. *Useful Plants of Tahiti*. Paris: Société des Océanistes, Musée de l'Homme, 1971.

Barrere, Dorothy. "Hawaiian Quilting: A Way of Life." *Conch Shell* 3 (1965).

Chabouts, L. and F. *Short Flora of Tahiti*. Paris: Société des Océanistes, Musée de l'Homme, n.d.

Cummings, C. F. *A Lady's Cruise in a French Man of War*. London: Blackwood & Sons, 1877.

Ellis, William. *Polynesian Researches*. 3 vols. Rutland, Vermont: Charles E. Tuttle and Co., 1969.

Gauguin, Paul. *Noa Noa: The Tahitian Journal*. New York: Dover Publications, Inc., 1985.

Hammond, Joyce D. *Tifaifai and Quilts of Polynesia*. Honolulu: University of Hawaii Press, 1986.

Holstein, Jonathan. *The Pieced Quilt: An American Design Tradition*. New York: Galahad Books, 1973.

Howe, K.R. *Where the Waves Fall*. Honolulu: University of Hawaii Press, 1984.

Keesing, Felix M. *Social Anthropology in Polynesia*. London: Oxford University Press, 1953.

Lehartel, Hilda. *Arts and Culture of Tahiti and Her Islands*. Papeete, Tahiti: Territorial Commission of Maohi Arts, Crafts, and Cultural Associations of French Polynesia, 1985.

Levy, Robert I. *Tahitians: Mind and Experience in the Society Islands*. Chicago: University of Chicago Press, 1973.

Mannering, Douglas. *The Art of Matisse*. New York: Excalibur Books, 1982.

Manu-Tahi, Chief Teriiteanuanua. *La Fleur Polynésie dans l'histoire et la legende*. Papeete, Tahiti: Les Éditions Veia Rai, n.d.

Mauer, Daniel. *Protestant Church at Tahiti*. No. 6. Paris: Société des Oceanistes, Musée de l'Homme, 1970.

Newberry, Colin. *Tahiti Nui: Change and Survival in French Polynesia, 1767-1945.* Honolulu: University of Hawaii Press, 1980.

O'Reilly, Patrick. "Note sur les 'tifaifai' Tahitiens." Paris: *Journal de Société des Océanistes 15* (1959).

Rae, Janet. *The Quilts of the British Isles.* New York: E. P. Dutton, 1987.

Turner, George. *Samoa, A Hundred Years Ago and Long Before.* Apia, Western Somoa: University of South Pacific, 1984.

Wheeler, Monroe. *The Last Works of Henri Matisse.* New York: Museum of Modern Art, 1961.

Acknowledgments

So many people helped to make this book a reality. The artisans and the associations who contributed their time, their help, and their tifaifai are too many to name individually. Some of the greatest kindnesses came from men and women whose names I never learned. I want to thank each and every artisan from the villages in Pirae and in Papeete for having patience with my many questions and for enduring my questionable French.

My special thanks to Tila Teuira Maziére, Chef du Service de l'Artisanat Traditionnel. Without her help and guidance, this book would have been impossible to research and to write. My special thanks also to Jacques Teuira, Territorial Government President, for his kind support.

I would also like to thank Stella Lehartel, president of the women's federation, for her assistance with our photographic needs.

For the use of the museum library and special insights about tifaifai, my thanks to Manouche Lehartel, Director of the Museum of Tahiti and the Islands.

A big thank you to André Teavai, from the Service de l'Artisanat Traditionnel, for the hard work, the translations, and the good company.

Much of the groundwork for this book was prepared by the staff and management of the Tahiti Tourist Promotion Board. My thanks to Christian Vernaudon, Patrick Picard-Robson, and Tiare Sanford.

And most of all, my gratitude and appreciation goes to the artisans who so freely shared their quilts and their history. Special thanks to Roura Tuhiti, Tehei Tuhiti, Marguerite Tapatoa, Ina Utia, Myrna Ti-paon, Lidi, and Pati Estall. Your gracious hospitality and your expertise made it all possible.

And, as always, thank you Lord Jesus.

Index

A

Ahu. *See* Mats
Ahufara, 18
Anthuriums, 98
Antique quilts, absence of, 9-10
Appliqué, 16, 18, 28, 34-37;
    floral, 29
    freestyle, 29, 44, 47, 51
    Rarotongan-style, 11, 28, 29, 44, 64
    snowflake method, 34
    Tahirihiri-style, 40, 95
Arii, 15, 35
Austral Islands, 8, 15, 32

B

Baby mats, 21
Baby tifaifai, 22, 75
Bastille Day observations, 22
Birth and birthday celebrations, 21-22
Bligh, William, 14, 60
Bora Bora, 10, 16
Breadfruit, 60
Bougainvillaea, 7
Broderie perse, 18

C

Christmas festivities, 22
Color sense, Tahitian, 7, 29, 91
Communal work, 17
Competitions, quilting, 23-24, 26-27, 51
Cook, James, 14
Cook Islands, 8, 44, 46

Cotton, availability of, 15
Crib quilts. *See* Baby tifaifai

D

Duff, H.M.S., 14

E

Ellis, William, 16, 18
Embroidery, for edges and definition, 28, 44, 51
Exhibitions, quilting, 23-24

F

Fabrics, contemporary, 19
Family designs, 18
Floral influence, 7, 9, 18
Frangipani, 7, 42
French, influence of, 18
Funeral rites, 22

G

Gauguin, Paul, 7, 8, 29, 95

H

Hammond, Joyce, 9
Hawaiian Islands, 8, 15
Hawaiian quilting, 11, 15
Heis, 8, 41, 77
Hexagons, 16
Hibiscus, 7, 56

I

Iripiti, 81

M

Maro, 91
Marriage festivities, 21
Matisse, Henri, 29-30
Mats, fine, 13, 14, 21, 22
Medallions, 44, 105
Men as designers of tifaifai, 24, 25
Missionaries, wives of, influence of, 8, 14, 15, 17, 73, 105
Moorea, 9
Mosaic, pieced, 30, 32, 81

N

New Year's festivities, 22
Niue, 8

O

O'Reilly, Patrick, 9, 16

P

Pa'a honu. *See* Hexagons
Painted tifaifai, 9
Pa'oti. *See* Appliqué, snowflake
Papeete, 10, 19, 23
Pareu cloth, 22, 32, 51
Patchwork, 16, 17, 23, 28, 30-33
Patterns:
    Anthuriums, 98-103
    Aute, 56-59
    Barn Raising, 30, 33
    Bear's Paw, 30
    Breadfruit, 1, 34, 60-63
    Cabbages, 68-71
    Chinese fan, 40
    Chou, 68-71
    Drunkard's Path, 30
    Fans, 35, 90-93
    Fe'i, 47
    Fetia, 30
    Flowers and Vines, 39
    Frangipani, 42
    French eagles, 35
    Gardenias, 76-79
    Hei Tiare, 104-107
    Hibiscus, 56-59
    Honeycomb, 30
    Horoi, 17
    Joseph's Dream, 112-15
    Lamp, The, 94-97
    Liane de Cyre, 19
    Lili, 32
    Log Cabin, 30, 33
    Meherio, 36, 37
    Mermaids, 36, 37
    Orchide, 30, 80-86
    Pa'aro, 28, 30
    Painapo, 38
    Patu, 30, 33
    Pineapples, 38
    Pu, 33
    Pua, 34, 41, 43
    Pua Mahana, 69
    Pūpū, 108-11
    Rimarima, 30
    Robbing Peter to Pay Paul, 30
    Roses, 64-67, 86-89
    Roti, 64-67
    Sawtooth, 30
    Sea, The, 40
    Star of Bethlehem, 30
    Sunflowers, 60
    Sunshine and Shadow, 30, 73
    Tahirhiri, 36, 90-93
    Taratara, 31
    Te Miti, 40
    Te Moemoea No Iotefa, 112-15
    Te Mori, 94-97
    Te Vahine e Te Miti, 50-55
    Tiare, 46
    Tiare No Maire, 105
    Tiare Opuhi, 10, 34, 44, 45

Tiare Tahiti, 76-79
Tiare with Vines, 39
Tifaifai Pu, 72-75
Tipani, 42
Trip around the World, 73
Triton's Trumpet, 109
Uru, 1, 34, 60-63
Vines, 42
Woman and the Sea, The, 50-55
Pillowslips, 9, 31
Pirae, craft village, 10, 12
Pomare II, King, 16
Printed (patterned) fabrics, 9, 32, 44
Pu. *See* Patchwork

Q

Quilting, origin of in Tahiti, 8-9

R

Raiatea, 81
Rarotonga, 8, 21, 22, 46
Rarotongan-style quilts. *See* Appliqué
Roses, 64, 87
Royal patterns, 17-18, 35
Rurutu, 8, 21, 22, 32, 81

S

Sailors, influence of, 8
Samoan Islands, 13, 15, 21

Secrecy regarding quilt patterns, 18-19, 30-31
Society Islands, 42, 91

T

Tahiti, 14, 21, 22
Tapa, 13, 14, 15, 18, 21, 22, 91
Templates, 20
Tiare Aute. *See* Hibiscus
Tiare Maohi, 77
Tifaifai:
  ceremonial purposes, 21-22
  sale of, 22-23
  See also Appliqué; Baby Tifaifai; Patchwork
Tiputa, 18, 22
Tivaevae. *See* Appliqué, Rarotongan-style
Tongan Islands, 14, 15
Transferring patterns, 24-25
Tuamotu Islands, 39, 81
Tubuai, 8
Turkey-red, 16, 91

V

Vehiturua. *See* Pillowslips

W

Whaling captains, wives of, influence of, 8